Turnabout:

NEW HELP FOR THE WOMAN ALCOHOLIC

T0163104

Turnabout:

NEW HELP FOR THE WOMAN ALCOHOLIC

Jean Kirkpatrick, Ph.D.

Fort Lee, New Jersey

Published by Barricade Books Inc.
Fort Lee, NJ 07024
www.barricadebooks.com

Printing History:
Madrona edition published 1986
Bantam edition / 1990
Barricade first printing / 1999

Copyright © 1977, 1978, 1986 by Jean Kirkpatrick
All Rights Reserved.

No part of this book may be reproduced, stored in a retrieval system, or transmitted in any form, by any means, including mechanical, electronic, photocopying, recording, or otherwise, without the
prior written permission of the publisher, except by a reviewer who
wishes to quote brief passages in connection with a review written
for inclusion in a magazine, newspaper, or broadcast.

Library of Congress Cataloging-in-Publication Data
Kirkpatrick, Jean.
    Turnabout: new help for the woman alcoholic / Jean
    Kirkpatrick.
        p. cm.
        ISBN 1-56980-146-0
        1. Kirkpatrick, Jean. 2. Alcoholics—United States—
Biography. 3. Alcoholics—Rehabilitation—United States—Case
studies. 4. Women—United States—Alcohol use—Case studies. I.
title.
    HV5293.K47A3 1990
    362.29'2'092—dc20
[B]   89-17726
                                                    CIP

Tenth Printing Barricade
Printed in the U.S.A.

PREFACE

Turnabout is a book about despair and hope. It is the story of my uncontrollable drinking and its glorious cessation. My recovery saved my life. I was so grateful to have it back that I wanted to share my methods with women for whom nothing else has worked, and who are desperate to survive. What came of my effort was the first women-oriented program for recovery.

In 1978, when *Turnabout* was first published, the idea of a separate treatment for women based on the premise that their needs in recovery differed significantly from those of the male alcoholic, was unheard of. Prior to this, the program of Alcoholics Anonymous was administered indiscriminately to male and female. Should an alcoholic declare that he or she couldn't get sober with AA it was concluded that the problem lay with the alcoholic, not the program.

But AA does not meet the needs of everyone, and specifically does not meet the needs of women. Fewer than 3% of women alcoholics are in AA. Surely women need something more.

My belief that men and women require different approaches to sobriety inspires my Women for Sobriety program. It has helped thousands of women recover. The program recognizes that sobriety depends very strongly upon self-esteem, which is only reclaimed through feelings of value and self worth.

I want women to learn their strengths and to become aware that they are competent. Only then does their struggle with alcohol become a fair fight. In our patriarchal society, many women have become vulnerable to dysfunctional relationships or traumatic life experiences that encourage a distorted sense of themselves. They feel underconfident or simply "not good enough." This is a huge drawback in the shaky first few months of recovery when personal strength is needed to fight addiction.

Once one resolves to live without alchohol one understand that one must find constructive ways to cope with one's problems. This presents special problems for some women. They will be afraid to take control of their lives if they have never known they were competent and able to accomplish whatever they choose. During my recovery I was transformed by the realization that goals are acceptable, and should be seen as *dreams with a deadline.*

Particularly for a woman, gaining a healthy sense of entitlement is crucial to attaining sobriety. Housewives, mothers, and professionals (most are a combination of all three) are constantly in demand and can lose themselves all too easily.

It is essential for the female alcoholic to stop waiting to be happy "someday" and start enjoying life right now.

Turnabout works toward that end. It has changed lives and it can change yours. The ideas in these pages confirm what you already know—that unless you do something about your problem it will bury you—and provide a framework for turning your life around. Once you promise yourself you will overcome this very difficult time, it can only get better.

JEAN KIRKPATRICK, PH.D.

WOMEN FOR SOBRIETY, INC.
P.O. Box 618
Quakertown, PA 18951-0618
Phone: 215-536-8026
Website: www.womenforsobriety.org
e-mail: newlife@nni.com

Chapter 1

Thank God it was time for lunch. My head was splitting and I was very edgy. Better look for someone. Bob? Bryan? No, neither one ever had a cocktail before lunch. Betty? Absolutely.

It was only a little past eleven in the morning but I decided that I should go to early lunch so that the others could go at the regular time. Anyway, I was at a good stopping place. Actually, I hadn't really started yet. But a good lunch would fix that.

Looking across the large office, I caught Betty's eye and, pointing to my watch and making a motion as if I were lifting a glass, raised my eyebrows in question. She broke into a big smile, grabbed her handbag, and came to my desk.

"I thought you'd never ask!"

Laughing, I grabbed my handbag and off we went, happy with anticipation of what was to come.

"Pelligrino's?" I asked.

"Why not?"

The Italian place I named was known for its whopping drinks. The manhattans were served in brandy snifters and one could almost stand on the edge and dive in.

In no time we were there, seated and ordering our prelunch drinks. There had been little conversation between us before this transaction. Now we could relax and talk, since the most important contract of the day had been made.

"I just love coming to lunch early," Betty was saying, as the waiter put our drinks before us. We both reached for them at the same moment, before they hit the table to rest.

Taking a quick gulp, I agreed with her. I thought how good it felt to be sitting here and relaxing before getting back to the dull business of writing technical textbooks for unemployable adults whose reading "skills" were those of grade five. Although boring, the job paid very well. Unfortunately, the more I made, the more I spent so that I was constantly in debt and had to go on with the job. My most recent financial adventure was renovating an old farmhouse that needed everything except a roof.

"I'm ready too," Betty was saying to the waiter as he was taking my empty glass. I hardly noticed having emptied mine. "Where have you been?"

"Just thinking about my house."

"That again. Let's drink to it." Betty lifted her new drink in a salute. I followed suit.

"Shall we order?" I asked, hoping she would opt for one more drink.

"Oh, let's just have a quick one before we do."

We did, drinking it faster than ever because our lunchtime had run out.

"Well, there's always the sandwich machine," I said, but both of us knew neither of us would eat. "Shall we have one at the bar before we go back to the salt mine?" I asked, trying to sound casual. But I knew I didn't have to care with Betty. We both loved to drink and enjoyed our special kind of lunch hours and felt we owed no one an explanation, much less each other.

"Why not?"

We made our way into the darkened bar and avoided the men's glances. Neither one of us looked at any of them, too eager were we to get a last drink, which we did.

"Um, tastes good. Hate to go back."

"I know, but must. Let's go."

Not too steadily we left the bar and got to the car for the short drive back to our office, which was in a technical school at Wilkes-Barre, Pennsylvania, a depressing city. Our conversation was animated. I was so glad to be feeling better. In fact I felt like a million dollars and said so to everyone in the office as we entered the large room of desks in the front room of the school. Few were there, all taking their lunch hours at the proper time. I glanced at the clock and saw that we had been gone almost two hours. So what, I thought? Don't I give most of myself to this rotten job? They can just fire me if they want to. I don't really give a damn.

I moved hurriedly in the direction of the Xerox machine and suddenly fell over an office chair. For seconds I seemed to tumble with the chair, not able to stop my falling or the movement of the chair. Finally we both came to a halt and I tried quickly to stand but my foot had been badly twisted under me. Bob rushed to my side and helped me. Immediately my foot was swollen.

"Let me take you to the infirmary at the Wilkes-Barre hospital."

"No, Bob, it's quite all right. I'll drive home to my own doctor." Oh, if he'd only let me alone, I thought. Every minute someone else came to the scene and I felt myself getting extremely irritable.

Nick, my boss, suggested I go home and I decided that that was the best advice yet. "Are you O.K. to drive home?"

"But why not?" I asked defensively.

As hurriedly as I could, I gathered my things and left the office, saying good-bye to no one.

Getting into the car slowly, I thought of the long drive home on the turnpike, eighty-five miles. It would take almost two hours. Oh well, I have a bottle of Bourbon in the glove compartment if the pain gets too terrible, because now it was really beginning to hurt.

As I was leaving the city, I got the bottle from the glove compartment and took a healthy swig along with several aspirins. Then I leaned the bottle next to me as I drove. Thank goodness I always carried one with me for just such times as this. Planning.

The drive home, although long, really was quite bearable until the half pint was emptied. Then I drove faster and got to the doctor's office by 6:00 P.M. He took one look at my foot and began a series of X rays. Suddenly I felt great joy in knowing I wouldn't have to go to work tomorrow. I could stay at home and "relax."

By evening, enough friends knew of my plight and came to my rescue with a party. We celebrated the great news of my being home for several days. It was like a special vacation.

That evening passed on all too quickly. In fact, I remembered very little of it. By next morning, I awoke to great pain . . . in my head, my foot, my stomach. Everywhere. How could I have been so stupid to get such a helluva hangover? Oh yes, the party! Well, I thought, that's the end of parties like that for me. Never again! Maybe the rest like to drink like fools, but not me. Never again!

Right now, however, I decided I had better get myself put together so that I could get to the doctor's office for treatment. But, oh! getting out of bed was rough. Groaning, I managed to get to the bathroom and look at my bloodshot eyes. Terrible.

Didn't I remember seeing a bottle in the bedroom? I got it and poured a big shot into the fizzing Alka-Seltzer. That's the only way to get it down, I thought.

Not much happened after drinking the Alka-Seltzer so I poured another shot into the glass. I had a hangover, didn't I? Too darn much celebrating, that's what did it. Damn, why did I do it? I seemed to feel worse by the minute. Waves of nausea passed over me and I felt hot and cold.

I wanted to get to the doctor and knew I had to pull myself together no matter what. The only way I knew was to have another drink. And another. Ten minutes later I dressed myself and began to feel much better. I assured myself that I had really learned my lesson.

Hurriedly I left for the doctor's office, barely able to walk or drive, foot swollen to several times its right size. My doctor took me right into the treatment room and began with whirlpool.

"Aren't you hitting the sauce pretty heavily?" he asked me while examining my foot.

"Oh, last night everyone dropped in for a party," I answered casually.

4

"It seems to me that you had better slow it down. You look unrested. Let me give you a shot."

"No, I'm really O.K." His reference to a "shot" was because several weeks before I had had too much to drink and he came to the house to help me. But then I was probably getting a cold.

"This foot is bad," he was saying. "As soon as we can get the swelling down, it will have to be casted. Meanwhile, I'll have to see you daily."

"You mean I can't go to work?"

"Not making that long drive on the turnpike, you can't."

"Great!" I couldn't conceal my joy.

As I left the office, my foot really began to hurt a great deal, so I decided that I *had better* get to the liquor store so I could have a drink when the pain got unbearable.

At the liquor store I decided I'd lay in a good supply since many of my friends would be dropping in to see me. So I bought several half gallons of rye and a few bottles of champagne and a bottle of scotch. Who knows how many might come? It really had been a long time since I could look forward to having friends in for an extended period of time.

Despite the pain in my foot from all the movement, I was as happy as a lark. I drove home quickly, smiling to think of my precious cargo. The biggest problem of my morning was to get my liquor supply into the house without dropping it.

But I managed that too. Oh, how good it was to be on vacation!

Thinking about who I would call, I made myself a nice big highball with ice and club soda and Seagram's. It tasted so good, I drank it quickly and made myself another, as I prepared to make phone calls to disseminate the news of my being home. Oh, life was rich, life was sweet!

The day somehow slipped away while I made phone call after phone call. Of course, I talked to everyone for hours. It was so great being at home and not worrying about the job. At 4:00 P.M. I was surprised to see John and Sally drive in. Seems like I had called them earlier to come to dinner! Well, no matter, we'd manage something. Meanwhile:

5

"Let me get you a drink. It's been so long since I've seen you," I exclaimed.

"But we were here last night," Sally said.

"I mean to really *talk*." Were they here? Oh, that's right. I was celebrating! Oh well . . .

While Sally and John were talking to me, Mary and Phillip and Tammy came.

"I'll make the drinks, Jean. You're in high gear."

"You bet. Just keep them coming. We've got to celebrate my vacation."

The hours flew by. Sometime someone must have gotten pizza and even put me to bed. When I awoke in the early hours of the morning, I saw some pizza on the table next to the bed. It was half eaten. My clothes were all on but I was one big wrinkle.

In the darkness, I was suddenly very afraid. I began to perspire profusely and my heart began to thud like my head was thudding. Oh, why do I do it to myself? Why? I groaned audibly. I hated myself, everything about myself. I was loathsome, and I was lonely. And bored, and afraid and unhappy and very, very sad. Most of all, I was god-awful sick. I began dry retching and couldn't stop. Reaching out, my hand touched a bottle. Empty. I searched under the pillow and found one with some rye in it. Between retching, I gulped what was left. For a moment I thought I would vomit all over the bed.

Gradually I arose to a sitting position. If only I could call someone. I wanted to hear someone's voice.

But the room was pitch black and I began to shake. Wrapping my arms across my chest, I began to rock myself and moan. This somehow made me feel better. I had to get to the kitchen and get a big slug of whiskey but I was afraid to go. Leaning sideways from the bed, I turned on the table lamp. My head was splitting in two. Oh, God, help me, help me! Help me! I can't get a hold on myself. I'm lost. . . .

I started to go toward the stairway to get to the kitchen but my legs were paralyzed with fear. But I *had* to get there. Moaning and crying and praying, I inched my way down the now-lighted stairway. Help me get there, God. I *must* get there.

6

And then I was there, running now toward the bottle. All were empty. All the rye was gone! I began to get frantic. It couldn't be! But there stood the empty half gallons. Three of them. Suddenly I remembered the champagne. Ah, that was it. I opened the refrigerator door; the sight of the bottle lying on the shelf sent a wave of joy through me. I grabbed one and tore off the cap, champagne spilling over me and the floor. But I swallowed as much of the gushing foam as I could. Ah, heaven. That wonderful sensation of heat going through my body.

I drank as if my life depended upon it. It did. But I didn't know that. In minutes, I felt a thousand per cent better. Brother, that was close.

Taking the bottle with me, I went back to the bedroom and drank leisurely, for I had decided that I wouldn't drink today. Just recover this early morning. Sylvia was coming today and she always got angry when I drank. Huh, she had her bad habits too. Why should she always bug me about drinking? I had already decided to do something about it, hadn't I? That's what she wanted, wasn't it? She had seen me much worse when I first came out of the hospital, almost a year ago, where she was my psychiatric nurse. Comparatively I was much, much better now. No comparison and she should remember that.

But I decided to get into shape before she came. I wanted company.

Feeling so much better, I decided to snooze away.

Sylvia was standing beside the bed looking at me closely when I opened my eyes.

"Hi. Glad you're here." I had some trouble focusing.

"How are you feeling?" she asked while she inspected my foot. "This looks terrible. You'll be home for a while."

"Good."

I was feeling terrible. I had to have a drink. Actually I was still drunk but made a good show of being sober.

"I'm not staying. Just came to see how you were." She began to leave the room.

"But you said you were going to spend the evening," I exclaimed, disappointment in my voice. I felt let down.

"Why stay? You don't need me. You have your bottle."

7

"Thanks a lot." I was angry and insulted. Who did she think she was anyway? I reached for the bottle and drank defiantly. Now I didn't have to hide it from her. But I was sick, sick, sick. I must have looked that way too, for she was saying:

"Why don't you stop? Get with it?"

"I want to, you know that."

"But how can you if you keep on drinking? You've got to stop!"

"O.K. I'll call AA. Right now." I had really been wanting to. Now I felt self-righteous about it. "How about that? Will you go with me?"

"No."

"But why? You're always after me to do something about my drinking. Obviously you really didn't mean it." I knew I had trapped her with this always successful game of put-down.

"Look, Jean, you know I want you to go. But you're drunk now."

"So what? That's when you're supposed to go. I know all about it. Remember, I was in AA for three years."

With that, I called and finally got to talk to someone, a man who didn't sound too friendly. But he said they would pick me up for a meeting in Allentown, twenty miles away. They would arrive in a half hour.

I got scared. I didn't want to go. Having made the commitment, I began to rebel. I refused to change my clothes or comb my hair.

It seemed hours before they arrived. We had one heck of a time getting into the car, for there were four there already.

The man introduced himself as Jerry, and I disliked him immediately. I could feel that he wasn't crazy about taking us.

Looking at me, he observed, "You're drunk." There was no compassion in his voice and I immediately resented him.

"So? I thought AA was for drunks. Or has it changed since I was a member thirteen years ago?"

He said nothing more.

In this mood of disgruntlement, we made the twenty-mile journey to Allentown. The others ignored us, Sylvia and me. The enmity was overwhelming but we were on the way and had to go through with it. The car was very hot with all our bodies so close to each other and the heater going. I began to perspire and shake, needing a drink desperately. I was stuck, feeling nasty and angry because they were ignoring me. Call AA for help? Sympathy? It had sure changed.

Not much of that meeting sticks in my mind except the clannish friendliness of the people, who generally ignored us. Jerry seemed to be the leader and because he dismissed me, the others did the same. A woman came to me after the meeting and said she knew that I could really lick my problem if I got with the program.

"I know the program and it might work for some but it sure hasn't worked for these people," I said in the most insulting way.

She looked puzzled but I didn't explain my simmering anger for Jerry and his superego and power. I hated him.

Finally we left and drove home in silence except for Jerry's monologue to the others in the car, which excluded us.

When we got home I rudely said, as I got out of the car, "Thanks for nothing."

Jerry swore.

That night I wrote in my diary, "Most lives are long trails of debris and only death cleans them up."

After the fiasco with AA I decided that I would straighten myself out. Sylvia was again with me several days later. To Sylvia:

"Will you help me? I can't do it alone."

"Sure. I'll try to arrange a few days off from work. You're serious about it, aren't you?" She looked at me questioningly.

"Absolutely. I simply can't go on like this. I hate myself. I hate what I've become. And I'm so damn sick."

With that, Syl went to the phone and made inquiries as to when she could be away.

I took the opportunity to get to the closet in the living room where I had an emergency-supply bottle hidden. I was sick again. Green sick with waves of nausea coming over me. My hands shook badly. I had trouble drinking a gulp from the bottle. But I got it down. Then I felt sick all over again. All I could think about was getting over this siege.

"Wherever you are, stop drinking. I'll be here for three days. How's that?" Sylvia called from the telephone in the kitchen.

"That's terrific." I meant it when I said it, but I regretted asking her to stay, because the thought of not drinking was terrible. Yet I wanted to stop. Maybe I wanted to drink but just not be sick? Maybe that was it. Maybe.

"Look, I know you wish you weren't going through this and I do too, but let's do it. Today I'll give you a drink every once in a while. But you give me the bottle."

"I just can't do that. I feel like I'm all alone."

"O.K. You keep the bottle but no cheating."

I'd try but I really didn't see how I could manage. But I'd try.

"First we'll get you to the doctor for your foot. It looks terrible. Then we'll go to lunch. So let's get with it."

I was really happy to have someone be in charge. I felt like it would really be a snap this time. As I got ready to leave the house, I went quickly to the closet and had another gulp.

Sylvia was right behind me. "Look, either you are going to do it today or not. Which is it going to be?"

I felt as if I had betrayed her good nature. "Today," I said.

We were busy for the next two and a half hours and everything was going O.K. I ate some lunch but it tasted like sawdust. All I thought about was a drink. We ate in a diner that served no alcohol and I looked at all of the people, all just eating without a drink of any kind. How did they do it? All my thoughts were about alcohol and drinking. No matter what else I thought about, getting a drink was always uppermost in my thoughts. It was truly an obsession. It was more than that but I didn't want to think about that part. At least not now. All I wanted to do was to feel better but I was feeling like hell. My stomach seemed to be in Philadelphia and my head in New York. The rest of me was in outer space, where even the missiles would miss me. And my nerves were simply terrible. I wanted to scream, to run, to rant and rave, to break everything in sight.

"Let's go," Sylvia was saying, as she grabbed the check. "We'll go to a movie in Allentown."

"Please . . . I really can't go anywhere," I said imploringly. "I've got to have a drink."

"Not yet, in a little while."

"Now," I said emphatically, feeling my temper rise to terrible proportions.

"Look, are you going to do it this time?"

"Damn it, Sylvia, I've *got* to have a drink, *now*."

She saw my desperation.

"When did you have the last? Before we left the house?"

I nodded.

"That's only three hours ago."

"Look, I want a drink *now!* I've got to have a drink now. Or the hell with the whole thing."

"Threatening me won't do anything. We'll go over to that lounge and you can have as many as you want. I'm going home. I never liked being your keeper anyway. Call me when you're ready to come home. I'll send someone to get you."

With that, she left, taking the car and driving off.

I crossed the street, angry and happy. A drink. Thank God, I'd have a drink.

It was so dark I could hardly find an empty seat at the bar. I ordered and thought about Sylvia. Damn. When my drink came, I drank it quickly and went to a phone. Aw heck, she wasn't home yet. Guess I'll have another until she gets home. And I did.

Hours must have passed. There was Sylvia, talking to me. And I was sitting in a booth.

"Well, what are you doing here?" I asked, very surprised.

"Obviously I came for you."

"I called you but I couldn't get you. How did you know?"

"When did you call? Did you call? Or are you only saying that?"

"Honest. I called but you weren't home yet."

"Jean, do you know what time it is?"

"Afternoon I guess."

"It's two-thirty in the morning. The man wants to close but you wouldn't leave."

"But how could it be two-thirty?" I asked, thoroughly confused.

"It just is," she said while tugging at me to get up. I tried but had great difficulty. "Come on. We've got to go," she said with some impatience.

"I'm trying already, damn it."

The bartender came to help. Together they got me to the car. I began to sing. I really felt good. So what's wrong with having one too many once in a while?

"Look, Jean, will you knock it off? I'm tired and I could just scream."

"Well, you can go home any time you want to. Who asked you to baby-sit anyway? I'm sick and tired of you always telling me what to do. I had a damn good time and I had it all alone. But no, you had to come and take me away."

"Oh, shut up and sing," she said in contradictory exasperation.

"How can I shut up and sing?" I taunted. "You're really too much. You tell me to shut up and then you tell me to sing. Which do you want? See, there's no pleasing you."

I was tremendously pleased with my logic. And with myself. I had had such a good time tonight. Why the hell didn't she go home?

We pulled into the lane and I got out of the car. I was very unsteady but caught the fender of the car, hoping Sylvia hadn't noticed it. I didn't want her to think I'd had too much to drink!

"Look, you can go on home. I'm very happy you came today but as you can see, I'm O.K. In fact, I'd rather you didn't stay."

"I'm going, but an hour from now you'll wish I were here. Just don't call. You never intended to stop drinking."

"Guess not," I slurred. "I can handle it anyway. I just had two bad days, that's all. So long," I said rudely.

I staggered into the house and headed for the closet. And the bottle.

I awoke sometime during the next afternoon, sick, angry,

frightened, dispirited, filled with shame and so thoroughly disgusted with myself. Why did I continue to do it?

My head was splitting, my stomach was churning. Again I began with heaving, as though my stomach were trying to leave me. I began to moan and cry. I had to have help, but who? How? But, first, I had to try to get up. Finally I managed to get to the bathroom and wanted to throw some water on my face. When I looked at myself, I couldn't focus very well but the sight of myself filled me with rage and loathing. My fist lashed out at the mirror and broke it. Then I began to cry uncontrollably, blood dripping all over the sink from my cut hand, but I felt nothing.

As if out of the ether, Sylvia appeared. I felt a great rush of joy and love for her! I never was so glad to see anyone in my total life!

Without a word, she gently moved me toward the bedroom and got cold wet cloths for my hand. In minutes she had the blood stopped and my hand wrapped.

"I'm sorry. I'm sorry, I'm so sorry. Will you forgive me?" I couldn't remember much about the night before but I did remember her leaving after I went to the cocktail lounge to drink in the afternoon.

"Shhhhhhh. Lie down and try to rest. I'm not threatening you but this time you'll do it, I know."

"Yes, absolutely I will." Again I began retching. "I want to stop, you know that?"

"I know that but you also *must* stop."

I tried to look at her but I could not see her. A haze was over my eyes and everything was a blur. Lately I wasn't able to see in the morning after I had had too much to drink.

Sylvia was giving me some pills and orange juice. But that didn't stay with me very long. But, hour after hour, she persisted.

With the pills I was able to sleep. Somehow the day and night passed. A day later I began to eat soup and drink juice. But I really needed a drink. That's all I thought about, yet I knew there was nothing in the house and no way to get anything. Anyway, I wanted to stop *now*. Forever. Oh, I couldn't think about it.

"You look better. How do you feel?"

"Much better. Like I'm going to live," I said jokingly.

"For a while I didn't think you would," Sylvia said quite seriously.

I was shocked. "You're kidding?"

"No. You don't seem to understand what you're doing to yourself. It's no joke anymore. Your brain damage is obvious. You can't focus for days, your speech stays slurred. And the retching can cause hemorrhage in your esophagus, to say nothing of the paralysis of your breathing mechanism."

I was scared. A cold feeling stole over me. Somehow I knew that what she was saying was true. But why did I do it? Why? I shuddered. Never again. Never. Never. Never!

"Shall we do something today?" I asked Sylvia. She was so kind to me.

"I don't think so. One more day in bed and sleep. Maybe tomorrow. Have you thought about what you are going to do while you are home with your foot in the cast? It will probably be another several weeks before you drive on the turnpike."

Weeks. How wonderful! "Maybe I'll get to my dissertation. What do you think?"

"I think that's a good idea as long as you don't let yourself get discouraged and drink."

A long sigh escaped me. "I've just got to make it this time. I don't want to be that way. You know that, don't you?" I began to cry and couldn't stop. I felt exceedingly sorry for my miserable self. Why did this have to happen to me? Poor me?

Sylvia left the room while I wallowed in tears and self-pity . . . for three days more.

But then I began to feel like a million dollars, better than I'd felt for years. Most afternoons I'd have a splitting headache and feel washed out, but each day my headache came later. For a week I hadn't touched a drop. Sylvia was again working but each day after work she came and stayed overnight. Life was sweet. I began work on my dissertation but the work wasn't going well. My notes were cold. So much had been forgotten.

Hourly I lost my temper and thought about drinking. And I was beginning to worry about Thanksgiving, always several days of drinking. What the hell, maybe I'd have just one. But no more. Not after what I'd just been through. Never again would I suffer like that. Never, not in a million years.

But the dissertation bothered me. Ten years earlier I had passed my board examinations for the Ph.D. and had gone to celebrate. My dissertation was let go, although it had had a very good beginning. Now, however, it was almost foreign to me. My copious notes were just so many words on a piece of paper. Whenever I'd really try to get into them and understand what I'd written a decade earlier, I'd get very nervous; my hands got wet with perspiration and I had trouble breathing. Cold fear, but of what? Failure? But *not* doing it was certain failure. Or could I just dismiss it with saying I never got around to finishing it? That way I wouldn't really have failed, only postponed it. Everyone would buy that. But to finish it and have it rejected? *That* would be failure supreme.

Oh nuts, I'm going to have one drink.

Having made the decision, I drove to the liquor store as best I could with my one foot in a cast. The driving was unsafe, but I had to get there and did. My prudence showed in my buying only a half pint. Nothing could come from that.

I drove home with eager anticipation. When I got there, I saw Sylvia's car and my heart sank. What to do? She'd know where I had been. Might as well go face the music.

"Hi." I tried to act casual.

"So you've decided to go back to your misery?" she asked, with much disappointment in her voice.

I hated myself. I felt trapped. "I'm sorry. I just wanted to have one drink. I only bought a half pint. See." I pulled the small bottle from my handbag.

"Don't show it to me. I knew it was coming. Thanksgiving two days away. You always must celebrate the holidays, no matter what. Isn't that so?"

"Oh damn. I feel so trapped. What am I supposed to do?" I said with anguish.

"Look, Jean. You know what that does to you. Do you want to die that way or do you want to be happy and well?"

"But I won't get drunk!" I insisted.

"You can't really believe that," she said with exasperation. "You've been drinking all of your life and you have never stopped at one, *ever*."

"I'll prove it to you. I'll have one and throw the rest away!" I meant what I said, while I was saying it.

"No, I'm leaving."

"Please let me have one," I begged, like a willful child.

"You do what you want to do. I'm going. And this time I won't be back."

Suddenly I got very angry. I was begging to have a drink in my own house! Ridiculous.

"O.K., go. Have a nice holiday," I said sarcastically.

"Won't you be reasonable, Jean? Think about it. Think about being sick," she asked one last time.

"I won't be this time," I told her coldly. "I said I was going to have one and throw the rest away."

"So long."

She drove away and I felt relief. And a great sadness.

Slowly I walked into the house and fought the urge to drink. I put the sealed bottle into the cupboard and went back to trying to work on my dissertation. For thirty minutes I fought the hard fight but finally went to the kitchen cupboard and opened the bottle. With great care I poured a small amount into a glass and drank it neat. A great satisfying warmth crept over me and I felt myself smiling. *This* time I knew what I was doing and I remembered how sick I was last time. I thought about it and felt a sense of revulsion. Never, never again. Carefully I replaced the bottle in the cupboard and went back to work, happily certain of my control.

I forced myself to do sections of work I detested, especially following up on bibliographical notes. Now I made myself do it. And I stayed with it for almost an hour. Then I decided that I was so good, I could have another small drink.

All the time I was getting it, I congratulated myself on the wonderful way it was to feel, just drinking this way, a drink just every so often, just like regular people. The book said a person could manage an ounce an hour. Not bad. I could go all day like this.

As I drank I noticed that my half pint was looking very small and certainly going down fast. Tomorrow was Thanksgiving and I might have company. I decided that before getting back to work, I'd better get to the liquor store before the holiday crowd got there.

I finished my drink and drove to the liquor store. There I was faced with a dilemma. I didn't want to drink but I really had a lot of friends who always drank a lot. I decided I had better get a half gallon, maybe two.

As I left the store my mind was racing as I thought about who might come. The whole gang just might drop in.

At home, happily I stashed it away. What a nice warm feeling with a cupboard full of bottles of liquor. It gave me a great sense of security.

Before getting back to work, I decided to call Judy to come for a drink. The holiday feeling was beginning to overtake me.

While dialing I poured myself a short drink. I always enjoyed a drink while phoning.

To my surprise and delight, Judy could come . . . in an hour.

I was very happy. No more work for today. Ah well, I had done some, and that was the most important thing. Now to some play. Everyone deserves a holiday. And Thanksgiving comes only once a year. And I don't often see Judy.

I felt alive, like a million fires were lit inside of me. What could be better than anticipation?

While preparing some small sandwiches, I had a nice long highball, I certainly didn't want to blow it today. Tomorrow was Thanksgiving, and I was going to have a good time. Dinner with my family and relatives.

I felt so very happy. Preparing food was always a favorite pastime, especially for entertaining. As I reached for another drink, I saw I had to open the half gallon. So what? I had to anyway when Judy came.

It seemed like just minutes before she arrived. Oh, the joy!

The afternoon flew by. Sometime in early evening I remembered a house full of people, all having a great time. I wanted to remember something but time slipped by. I couldn't hold it in my grasp. Everything seemed kaleidoscopic.

Then the house was silent and I staggered through it. All the lights were burning. Stale cigarette smoke lingered and empty glasses were everywhere. Whiffs of liquor caught my nostrils and I felt violently ill. I felt green; waves of nausea passed over me. I had to get to bed, get some sleep, I told myself, but every time I lay down I was seized with terrible fear. Water seemed to pour out of the entire surface of my skin. I circled myself with my arms and rocked in the bed. I wanted to call someone but couldn't cross the room. Oh, God, how did it happen again? What did I do? Why?

I'd worry about that later. Now I had to get through this night. Could I call someone? I felt all alone in outer space. "Someone, please someone come by to see if I'm O.K."

Even in my stupor I knew no one would come by. No one . . . I felt very alone, as if I had always been alone in a world that no one could reach. I was in this world always and no one ever got close. I felt overwhelmed with my failures, my inability to cope with anything, my weakness, my physical misery, the shambles my life was in, and I felt very sorry for myself.

Nausea again seized me and I began the dry retching. I managed to sit upright and waited the necessary second or two for my brain to catch up with my new position. I felt like I was "flying apart" and my glazed stuporous eyes seemed to be watching me, unmoved, uncaring.

Half crawling, half walking, I got to the bathroom and tried to look in the mirror. For a moment there was no focus, but when I did see, staring at me was a yellow-green face of dissipation with wrinkled dry skin hanging loosely over the face, eyes glazed and without intelligence, creases of tension vertically above the bridge of the nose and horizontally across the entire forehead, the corners of the mouth cracked.

I began to sob. I wanted to die. The loathing I felt for myself was complete. I wanted to tear the new mirror from the wall as the rage engulfed me. Then I began to whimper, like the wounded animal I was.

Searching for a bottle in the bathroom and bedroom, I found none with any liquor. All were empty. But I couldn't get to the kitchen because of fear. Voices seemed to be off in the distance and I didn't want to know who they were. They were all talking about me.

Oh, I wanted to die, to be out of this misery.

Why not? This seemed like the right day. The thought brought great relief. No more suffering, no more sickness, no more fear. Never to be frightened and alone again. Oh, it was too much to be believed!

With a great effort I got to the bathroom and found the pills, the meprobamate. There were almost a hundred. I knew that twenty-five would do it. But I'd take them all.

As I began taking them, I had a great problem with swallowing them. It seemed like a half hour went by until I swallowed all of them.

But somewhere along the way, I knew nothing more.

Chapter 2

What could possibly drive a woman to drink to suicidal depression? What could make any woman drink with such total abandon, such complete surrender? Five million women are in this predicament. The disease of alcoholism is a crippling disease from which 450,000 children and 10 million men and women suffer. Of these adult alcoholics, less than 4 per cent are found on skid row. The remaining 96 per cent are making a stab at living normal lives with an abnormal problem. Very likely they are your friends or even yourself.

The woman alcoholic is not something new, only the recognition of her. Today the sheer number of women who suffer from alcoholism is equal to the populations of Maine, Idaho, Nevada, Montana, New Mexico, and Utah!

The woman alcoholic suffers not only from the illness of alcoholism but also from the additional stigma of its being "unladylike."

It is hard to know if alcoholism among women is on the rise. Drinking itself is now so socially ingrained that not to offer guests something to drink or even not to take an offered drink amounts to something tantamount to a social slur. All people drink more freely and more openly in the frenzy of this age.

Despite burgeoning populations, life today is lonelier than it ever was before. There is an impersonality that pervades society and its social institutions. There is every reason for us to feel helpless in the bleakness of this age of technocracy, this time of veneration for the gross national product.

Loneliness, psychiatrists and analysts claim, is the biggest problem among patients (not necessarily alcoholic) because few people know how to satisfy the deeper needs of life, the hungering of the soul for purpose. In the impersonality of the age, rarely do we think of ourselves against a backdrop of eternity. We live, instead, in a lonely world encircled by materialism and commercialism. This kind of cosmic loneliness brings about an alienation that is the perfect circumstance for excessive and solitary drinking.

Although loneliness may encourage drinking, it is not the cause of alcoholism. The cause still eludes scientists. Many women drink because of emotional reasons; only some become alcoholics. Only to some is this drug-addicting.

The image of the alcoholic woman has always been that of a woman boisterous, flirtatious, effusive, and sometimes loud-mouthed. This may be the person she sometimes becomes, but more often she is secluded in the privacy of her apartment or home after getting the kids off to school or after coming home from the office or classroom or clinic. She is shy, reclusive to a point (before telephonitis or visititis), alienated, retrospective, and lacking in self-esteem. Later in her drinking, she will become self-pitying, resentful, and even childishly cruel as a consequence of the drug, alcohol.

Alcoholism comes to a woman usually when she is in her late thirties or forties, often when her children are grown or when she is at the height of her career.

A woman drinks from a feeling of inadequacy and from a need for love, the kind of love that is not found within a sexual relationship but, rather, a love that is deeper and more primal. When a woman does not feel needed or when she cannot express this encompassing love, a sense of unworthiness possesses her and she ceases to care much about anything. Drinking fills an emptiness within self. Clara Barton, Florence Nightingale, and Jane Addams all filled this need with their great capacity for expressing love through prodigious work.

Sometimes this unfilled need is translated into drinking, but not every woman who drinks will become alcoholic. The woman who does turn to drinking to compensate for the emptiness she feels might be able to avoid the pitfalls of drinking if today's labor market would accept the mature woman. What woman over forty does not know the uselessness of seeking a job commensurate with her experience and ability?

Most drinking usually begins innocently enough with drinking at parties, celebrations, weddings, or other social occasions. This pattern may continue for a number of years. Gradually the addictive woman begins to drink just a little more than the others; she finds that the drinks aren't being served as fast as she would like them to be served. Often she will offer to help prepare them in order to get an extra drink while at the bar or in the kitchen. Or she might say, "How about another drink? I feel like celebrating tonight."

These declarations and actions become more and more frequent. It also leads to having cocktails with lunch or a drink before an interview or before meeting someone new or before going to a funeral or before any number of emotional experiences. One or two quick drinks provide the calming effect necessary to get through the occasion. Dependency is already present.

Soon the period arrives when she drinks *before* a party, *at* a party, and *after* a party. The compulsion to drink is now in full swing and her body is addicted to ever-increasing quantities of alcohol. Her body demands alcohol. It crowds out all other things from her mind; drinking has become an obsession. Now she visits only friends who offer her a drink; she has dinner in restaurants that serve cocktails. Her entire life is alcohol-oriented, but she is not aware of what is happening to her, as strange as that may seem.

Now, too, begin the awful hangovers. Sleep permits some of the alcohol to be oxidized, but the body craves more to replace it. Physical symptoms of withdrawal appear in the morning—shaking hands, perspiration, flushed face, a sense of uneasiness.

And so the morning drink begins. Just a half a glass of liquor and all the symptoms go away. But the subtlety and insidiousness go on. The alcoholic begins to change in ways she is never aware of. She becomes secretive about her drinking and cannot permit herself to know. There are many who carry on, year after year, just as if nothing extremely unusual is wrong with this kind of life. Many, in fact, carry on very well.

Recently, at a professional women's group meeting, I met a dynamic woman who was to receive our club's award for outstanding leadership. As a college president, this woman set many new records in administrative achievement.

During the cocktail period before dinner, I joined a small group that surrounded her. She was talking and laughing effusively, exuding a dynamism that attracted everyone to her. As I drank my ginger ale, I listened to her very carefully and I also noticed a very slight flush on her face. I knew it was not the flush of excitement, as others believed, but that she was, in reality, very drunk. Not one other person had the slightest suspicion.

I continued to watch her throughout the entire ceremony that night, and she managed it very well. But I also knew what the next twelve hours would be for her. She would leave the meeting and, when in her apartment, she would drink herself into insensibility. Why? Because she wouldn't be able to stop. The cycle of demand that knows no satisfaction had been set into motion. She would awaken the following morning, after only a few hours of sleep, shaking, depressed, promising herself never again.

But then to get the day started and the symptoms of withdrawal stopped, she would have to indulge in a morning drink before ever beginning to dress to get to work. In two hours, after the morning medicine had been applied in necessary doses, and had begun to work, she would be off to the campus. Almost no one would know the hell she lives in, for, outwardly, she appears quite normal to most.

Could this woman be you?

Alcoholics who are drunk yet operate in a seemingly normal way appear to others as merely animated, enthusiastic, filled with a zest for living that ordinary mortals seem not to have. This is, in fact, the greatest act in the world, one staged at an enormous price of studied calm and control. The alcoholic measures every gesture, every smile, mouths words precisely but with just the right amount of casualness.

As her disease progresses, the alcoholic woman stays more and more alone so as not to call attention to her drinking. She changes liquor stores in a desperate effort to keep store clerks from suspecting she drinks too much. Sometimes she will put empty bottles in other people's trash cans to keep trash collectors and apartment managers from knowing the truth. She begins to hide from her neighbors, while much of her day is spent in elaborate schemes of cover-up.

Drinking keeps the alcoholic woman busy; hiding it keeps her even busier. But she'll continue to say, "I'm not an alcoholic. Sure, maybe I drink a little too much once in a while, but . . ."

Perhaps the single most tragic part of alcoholism is that the woman with a drinking problem is the last to know. It is not that she is dull-witted. Rather it is because it is part of the disease, this inability to communicate the reality of what is happening to herself and her life.

Sometimes she will read or hear something about alcoholics and will file it into her subconscious, but it takes much, and great, tragedy before this information is brought out of the depth of her mind into operation.

Much of alcoholism's heartbreak lies in this resistance to knowing the truth, since nothing can be accomplished until the victim is able to admit the disease and want to do something about it.

Some women are alcoholics from the moment of the first drink, while others are not. Some women are daily drinkers, while others have long periods of time during which they do not drink. Which are the alcoholics? All of them could be.

Possibly the most reasonable description of an alcoholic is anyone who drinks uncontrollably at one time or another, no matter how long a time intervenes. One test for alcoholism is to set a limit of two drinks every time there is an occasion to drink. This should be exercised over a period of three months. The woman who can do this need read no further.

Many women feel certain they can pass this test and never

try. Not taking this test is a good sign of problem drinking in the offing.

But there are other telling signs. Women with a problem will say, "I really don't want a drink but if you're having one, I'll keep you company." Or, at a party, "How I dread that drive home. Do give me one for the road." Or when someone talks about a hangover, the alcoholic says, "I wouldn't know. It's been an age since I've had one." Hypersensitive to criticism, the alcoholic woman never permits herself to listen to those who caution her. Instead, she stays away ever more increasingly. Quite possibly her life is in ruins and those who love her have deserted her simply because they could not take any more squabbling and heartbreak.

Although feeling lost and alone and very frightened, she will go right on drinking because of not understanding what is happening to her. All she knows is that she can't live without drinking. She alone is the only one who thinks that her life will return to the way it once was. Just every once in a while she will have moments of thinking about asking for help. When very sick, she even occasionally thinks about calling Women for Sobriety or AA but then quickly puts it out of her mind, telling herself, "I'm not that sick. Those organizations are only for women with problems."

So she has a few more drinks to recover and manages to get through the day, with a drink here, another there, all nicely spaced until the evening, when she can drink with abandon and without guilt. This bad period is only temporary, she thinks, hypnotizing herself with the refrain of "the good old days."

Of course, they never return, those "good old days." For me, this was the very hardest thing to accept, that I could never drink again like I did in those "good old days." It was as if I were losing my most prized possession—this mania that got me into accidents, into jail, into hospitals, and into humiliating situations! This clinging to the necessity to drink, this belief that life couldn't be lived without alcohol, is often the factor that keeps alcoholics drinking. This is a major part of the disease.

I found it impossible to comprehend that other people lived

life without alcohol, that they lived from day to day without taking a drink. Now I find it equally hard for nonalcoholics to comprehend ever so slightly how the alcoholic's mind is possessed and obsessed with drinking. Who can understand this passion that leads a woman to sacrifice her family and her health in pursuit of the bottle? Why is it so difficult to give up an illness that tears a human being apart? What is so wonderful about feeling like hell most of the time? Who would want to be so endlessly concerned with the intricate details of where to get liquor, and how, and in the right amounts at the right times?

The woman with the disease of alcoholism.

Chapter 3

Someone was pushing me roughly and calling my name. I didn't want to open my eyes but finally I had to see who was irritating me. To my great surprise, it was my friend Bonnie, in her nurse's uniform. She was bending over me, shaking me.

"That's it, hon. You've had a close call. Wake up now and drink this."

She held a glass to my lips. I wanted to reach for it but found that I couldn't raise my arms. I was in restraints. My anger flared. Rage possessed me.

"Where am I? Why am I in restraints? Get me out. Get me out!" I screamed, on the verge of hysteria. "I want to go home . . . now."

"Shhhhhh. Just be quiet now. I'll get you out in a little while," Bonnie said soothingly. She smoothed the covers and put her hand on my forehead.

I felt panic sweep over me. This had happened to me several times in my life, where I had no control over my being or what I wanted to do, where I was subject to authority that kept me in restraint, where I was subject to the will and command of others. And getting out depended upon my displaying no anger, no rage, no emotion other than a calm sanity. When restrained like this, I knew gut fear. It had happened to me before, and to think that now, again, I was in restraints just like ten years before, but a different kind. Then it was handcuffs.

The ugly memory came back to me with vividness. I had passed my board examinations at the University of Pennsylvania in Philadelphia and had even received a first-time honor, first woman at the university to receive a Fels Fellowship, a real biggie. So happy was I with my great success that I decided to celebrate, to have a drink. Just one. How could it possibly hurt me when I had been completely dry for three years? Three years of AA and sobriety.

It was very hot that summer in Philadelphia. The day I received the notice about the fellowship I was living alone in an off-campus apartment and there was no one with whom to share the good news, which had come to me by telegram.

Reading it, I could barely contain my excitement. I wanted to shout the news to everyone within earshot. I felt an overwhelming gratitude for those men who thought me capable of such scholarship, so much so that they wanted to pay me handsomely while I wrote my dissertation.

With the telegram clutched in my hand, I ran to the small corner grocery store at the corner of Thirty-seventh and Market and bought a case of Fels liquid detergent.

At the cash register, Al asked, "You going to do a lot of washing?"

A big grin swept over my face. "Look." I thrust the telegram at him. "No more worry about money. And I'll have all the time in the world to do my dissertation!"

He read it slowly, probably not really grasping its significance but reacting to my joy.

"That's wonderful. Now you can stop worrying."

He knew that I had struggled during the last several years, trying to live on $5.00 a week food money while doing research for the books some of my professors were writing.

I went to pay for the Fels but hadn't the money. We both laughed.

"Can I give you a check for this? You know it will be good."

He smiled. "Of course."

So I lugged my case of Fels liquid detergent to my apartment. But I wasn't satisfied inside of me. I wanted to *feel* my victory, share it. Right across the street from the grocery store was a Negro night club, the Cobra Club. Why not go there for one drink? It was the middle of the day and I didn't want to buy a bottle, because I'd finish it and I certainly wouldn't stay for more than one drink across the street, because of fear and being out of place. Never had I done anything like that before but now my new victory seemed to make me invincible. And I could think that I was doing a sociological study. How do blacks drink in the middle of the day?

I began to be excited about having a drink after all of these years. I knew it would be a "slip" but now I knew where to go for help, if I needed it. But why think of that? I would have one and, after three years of sobriety, I knew I'd handle one. Sure, I might crave more, but I knew I couldn't drink them, because then I'd be in deep trouble and that's exactly what I now wanted to avoid with my new fortune.

Yes, I'll have one drink there. Since I'd never stay there, I felt I had a built-in security.

I crossed the street and hesitated several minutes before opening the door. My heart was pounding with excitement. Going in, it took me many moments to get my eyes adjusted to the darkness. Finally I saw that there were only a few black men at the bar and a bartender. All looked very startled as I took a seat in a booth.

When the bartender came to the table, I ordered very matter-of-factly.

"Seagram's and soda, please." I didn't look directly at him but close to his face.

Seconds later I had it and drank it greedily. It was ambrosia but not nearly enough. The drink was very small and very weak. I suspected I wasn't drinking Seagram's at all. Not wanting to make him come to the table again, I took my glass to the bar.

"Double Seagram's and soda, please."

All conversation ceased while my drink was being made. Since this was a sociological experiment, I looked at the men, smiled, and made some small talk. They were aloof.

Back to the table I went with my drink. I thought I drank it slowly, but it, too, was soon gone and my money was getting

29

low. Before, when I stood at the bar to get my drink, I noticed a big sign behind the bar, done crudely in crayons, as if it were changed frequently: "4 Corby's for $1.00."

What a bargain! I wrestled with myself. I was about to leave but I still had a dollar left. Why not blow it too? What the hell! I'd already had my slip.

I took my empty glass back to the bar and took a seat, ordering the four Corby's. Soon I was talking to the bartender. Then there were lots of people. And a nice black woman sat next to me for hours and talked, sometime in the night introducing me to her son, who was in the Air Force.

Sometime in the early morning, three of the men and the old woman took me home and laid me on the bed in my apartment.

And the next day began the continuation of the odyssey begun the afternoon before in celebration of my acknowledged scholarship and intelligence.

Days and nights became a blur of the sameness of clubs in mid-city, sometimes finding drinking companions and sometimes not. My checks had begun coming for my supposed dissertation writing and every cent went into the self-destruction of trying to find the most off-beat and off-limits clubs any city has to offer, all evidently police-protected because we always knew when there was to be a raid and stayed away that night.

Surely I was protected by more than the police, wandering around Center City side streets, drunk, going from one club to another invariably alone, sometimes sleeping in the car in a downtown parking lot. . . . It was inevitable that I would be caught by the police. Trouble came one night when I was very drunk and couldn't manage getting into my car. Apprehended, I was incensed that the policeman thought I needed help. We tussled for a while and I found a great amount of strength, that kind known to those trapped. I hit the policeman often; he finally subdued me angrily and put handcuffs on me, making them very tight, so that they bit into the flesh on my wrists. I swore.

In minutes I was carted off to City Hall in a paddy wagon and spent the rest of that night in jail.

I was very frightened. I knew that feeling of being in trouble and being alone. . . .

"Bonnie, I want to go home. I must go home. I can't stand it here." I whispered imploringly, fear choking every word. "Please, Bonnie, you're my friend. See that I get home."

"Soon, hon. But rest for now." She patted the covers, then smoothed my brow.

"What day is it? How did I get here? What happened?"

"Sylvia found you and called the ambulance. Dr. Miller and Dr. Kramer worked on you most of the night. You have been very sick. Your heart stopped several times. You are very lucky."

That really made me sore. Lucky?

I began to thrash around in the bed as best I could, trying to break the restraints. A nurse came in and was angry.

"You'd better simmer down or we will really tie you down."

I had run into this resentment before. Nurses and doctors hate taking care of patients who attempt suicide. The hell with her, I thought. But I started to give in to the terrible exhaustion I felt. My mind was muddled and my head was splitting.

"Bonnie, I want something for this headache. *Now.*"

"Sorry, pal. Nothing for you for a couple of days."

"Then I'm going home. And I'm going now."

"How?" she asked with reasonable logic. "Your foot is still in the cast."

Soon I drifted into sleep and didn't awaken again until the next day.

By that time I had made everyone miserable enough so that they permitted my discharge. Sylvia came to take me home.

I was more depressed than I ever remember being, to such a degree that I could not be civil to the one person who showed her care and concern for me. I wallowed in self-pity. It seemed to be more than that. I simply couldn't see any reason for living. I fought back tears and I seemed overcome with fear again. So deep was I into my own miseries and woes that I heard not one word Sylvia was saying to make me feel better.

We drove into the lane and the house looked like one I had never before seen. In fact, everything was unreal. Again I had the feeling of watching this all happen to someone else. Even being with Sylvia didn't give it a sense of reality, as was usually the case. She had been with me through so much that I usually felt a sense of security when she was at hand. But not this time. She seemed almost unreal to me. My feelings were very strange. I didn't feel like a person but merely a collection of parts that weren't functioning together. One merely watched the other.

When we got into the house I was overwhelmed with depression and despair. Oh God! help me to overcome this nothingness, this awful despair, this self-loathing.

"Why don't you lie down and I'll fix us a sandwich."

The house looked so unfamiliar it seemed not to belong to me. I was very confused and felt as if I had been dropped into someone else's home. I walked around and touched this chair and then a table, yet unable to make a mental connection.

As I sat down, my eye caught the sight of an empty bottle that had fallen behind a chair across from me. Suddenly it struck me that this would have been the day of my funeral. Sobs caught in my throat.

Sylvia came into the room with the plates of sandwiches. Wordlessly she put them down and balanced herself on the edge of my chair while gently rubbing my back.

This was surely one of the low points of my life. There had been others but not many like this.

I cried until on the verge of exhaustion and collapse. Sylvia helped me to bed.

Several hours later I was feeling better. Just empty.

"You look better. How do you feel?"

I could feel my weak smile that resisted facial muscles. "Better."

Sitting upright, I knew I was feeling better. "I really feel much better, thanks to you." I wasn't quite so disoriented.

She reached over and squeezed my arm reassuringly.

"This time you've got it made. I know it. And this afternoon or tomorrow the cast will be taken off your foot. I'm going to work now but I'll be back. In the meantime, Lucy and Mary will be here to see you."

Quickly shuffling the cover and sheets in the way only nurses do, she said, "I must run." I knew she was doing this purposely. Testing me, giving me a chance.

I got out of bed to see her off. My legs were weak and my head was not my own. Standing at the door, I watched her drive out of the lane. And I wondered why I couldn't be like other people . . . go to work and not always feel upset and disgruntled and disgusted and depressed and self-loathing? Maybe the secret was not to think about anything except just that. Maybe I expected too much. But there was a tiger inside me, driving me to hell's end. Something ripped at me, chewed me up, and never let go. Even now, at this moment, the churning was starting. I wanted to run away. I wanted a drink. I wanted to be drunk. I wanted to be dead. I wanted no part of the life I had, yet, to many, it seemed quite attractive . . . good job, big old farm with an immense barn and acreage, parents, many friends. You have it all, Jean, everything but peace of mind and happiness.

I looked at the fading sunset this November day and thought only in morbid terms, seeing the crucifixion of the sun as the death of another day.

I sat in a chair; time slipped by unnoticeably. My mind drifted until Lucy and Mary came. Although they stayed for hours, I hardly kept abreast of the conversation. I was pleasant but one part of me was watching the other. All I wanted was a drink. My body screamed for a drink.

Finally they left, after much protestation of wanting to stay the night. Seems Syl had suggested they do, but my arguments, as well as the fact that it was my own home, prevailed. I was not in the mood for small talk, although I knew it was a way out of the tunnel.

I knew it would be a long night so I turned on every light in the house and got myself set in front of the TV. No matter what came on the channel I had it turned to, I watched and forced myself into absorption. It was a way to blot out "drink." I knew there was not one drop in the house, not even Listerine, to which I had frequently resorted, or Jean Naté. And all stores were closed. I knew I could probably get it from the taxi driver, who usually kept a fifth in his cab for people like me. People like me? You mean alcoholics like me.

My gaze became more fixed on the screen. My mind paralyzed itself. Later I was awakened by the insistent ringing of the phone. It was minutes before I could gather my consciousness. Slowly I got to the phone, knowing it would be Sylvia. And it was. She was coming to get me for the occasion of cast removal.

A large sigh escaped me before I could assess myself. This day seemed brighter. The sun was streaming in the east windows. It was almost 10:00 in the morning. I walked from room to room, putting out the lights, glad that the night was over and everything seemed normal again. It was as if I had returned from a long trip into the darkness of nowhere. For a while, I thought I had a one-way ticket. I decided to grab my life and get it going again. Upward and onward. Forget the past. Hang in there today. But, oh, I could do it so much better with a drink!

Damn it, Jean, remember how sick you were. And depressed. And on and on and on and on, ad nauseam.

I really began to feel O.K. And I was hungry, very hungry. When Syl gets here, I'll take her to lunch. Meanwhile, I called Nick at the office and announced my arrival on Monday. He seemed happy that I would be back. Inwardly I groaned when I thought about the turnpike each day but not for long. There were rumors that our government grant would not be renewed. Although I'd be out of a job, I would be happy that this particular one was over. But it probably wouldn't happen. There had been rumors from the time I began. So, what the hell . . .

Meanwhile I repaired to the bathroom and began to reclaim myself. A bath and hair wash and general overhaul began to show some results. Except for a splitting headache and some slight tremor in my hands, I felt better than I had for a month. Looking at myself finally, I saw that I still looked somewhat sallow and there were still some circles under my eyes, but I was on the way back. Seemed like every time recently, it took longer to get back . . . back to the world of others and back to feeling like a people's person.

Well, I thought, life isn't so bad if you just don't think about anything. Stick with the immediate: go to the cleaners, do the wash, get groceries, or, in the phrase of one who should know, vitalize the vicissitudes. That's it, Jean. Gee, maybe I could print that in large letters, or have it engraved on bathtubs. That's where my fortune might lie.

"Hi, I'm here," Syl called.

I limped down the steps. "See. I am again humanized."

She smiled broadly. "It's so good to see you this way. Terrific, in fact."

That day with Sylvia was probably one of the nicest days I had enjoyed in the past several years. My mind was still preoccupied with thoughts of drinking and my body occasionally rebelled, but I managed very well and began to feel put together. I forced the focus of my mind.

Everywhere we went, I saw crowds of people not drinking and I still could not understand how they managed to live that way. Of course, Sylvia steered me into places that didn't serve liquor, so that accounted for most of the "phenomenon." But it still seemed unbelievable that so many did not indulge and seemed not to mind it.

Purposely I made my life hectic. I thought I was keeping busy but I was running away from myself, yet that thought never crossed my mind.

My job was writing technical textbooks for unemployable adults and this sometimes took me to the school where we were training them, in Wilkes-Barre, Pennsylvania. It was a beautiful but long trip north on the Pennsylvania turnpike. Repetition was boring and I drove it at least four times a week. My company, Educational Computer, paid my weekly motel expenses and, usually, I drove to Wilkes-Barre on Monday morning, staying at the Holiday Inn overnight and then driving home after work on Tuesday. Before getting home, however, I stopped in Bethlehem for my class at Lehigh University. This pattern was again repeated on Thursday and Friday. Midweek, on Wednesday, I took the turnpike south and went to the home office in King of Prussia, a suburb of Philadelphia, almost sixty miles. Sometimes I left work early to go in to the

University of Pennsylvania library to check some of the notes on my dissertation, for I was again struggling with it.

Following a pattern in my life, I enrolled for six graduate credits at Lehigh University for graduate work in administrative education, a field of endeavor I knew absolutely nothing about. Challenges of any kind kept me in line, so I now chose one that verged on the possibility of real failure for me. When I attended my first graduate class, I was certain that my academic doomsday was at hand. I was the only one in the class from a different discipline and it was as if I had dropped in from Mars, for the others and for me. During the first several weeks I understood very little so unfamiliar was I to the educator's language of "consortiums," "implementations," "modalities."

I was completely dazzled by this world that obviously existed but of which I never was aware. That I had a challenge on my hands was a serious reality.

Classes were dull and I had to keep myself from falling asleep. But I dreamed of becoming a dean of women or perhaps an officer in a women's college. I knew that my current job was without future.

Part of the reason I took classes was also to meet new people but I found no one particularly interesting. One of the men, a dean of an exclusive girls' school, asked me to go for a drink several times but I was not about to get involved in what he had in mind.

Although I was very lonely and knew that my life needed someone to love or I had to find a cause to live for, I simply did not need the headache or the heartache of a brief entanglement. I was seriously looking for someone with whom to share the rest of my life. To my dismay, every man in class was married but that seemed to make little difference to them. This in itself disgusted me . . . their cavalier attitude toward their marriages and their wives.

But this situation was not the least bit new to me. As a divorced woman, men always reacted in just one way: they viewed themselves in the role of servicer to the lonely divorcée.

My attitude toward men in general was never very good nor

very bad. They were just there and I never reacted one way or another, perhaps because I was always popular enough. There was never a time when men were not trying to be involved. But from my divorce onward, my attitude toward men in general changed. I became always aware that men are, in the first place, sexual.

And somehow I was smart enough now to know that an involvement would be disaster. It always had been when I lived at the farm and in the small town of Quakertown.

Besides all of that, I had made my life so full I had little time to get to the places I was scheduled to be. The days became a blur of routine. Some days my drinking was in excess but I worked hard at keeping some control.

MARCH 2
Drank all day. Mother had my birthday dinner.

MARCH 3
Drove to Wilkes-Barre. Got there at 8:00 A.M. Snowing most of the way. Felt terrible. Worked with instructors until 5:30. Went to dinner with Bob and Vito. Then we worked in P.M. until 9:00. We all went for dinner and had a few drinks. Company had reserved a room for me at Holiday Inn. Watched news.

MARCH 4
Got up early and got to school at 7:45. Worked hard on instructors' manuals. Left W.B. at 3:00 P.M. Got home and fed the dog. Syl had yesterday. Hurried to class. Afterward, went to see Daddy at 10:30. Then home and watched TV until 1:00 A.M. Lonely.

MARCH 5
A real lousy day. Went to Dr. Esayian's before going to Stratford. Had a very upsetting letter from my dissertational advisor. He doesn't like my work. I feel empty and lost and hopeless and lonely and defeated. Only stayed in Stratford four hours. Feel like everything is collapsing around me. Tomorrow I go to Wilkes-Barre for two days.

What a life. Want to live in a sun country . . . Calif. or Fla.

MARCH 6
Left for W.B. at 6:00 A.M. Worked hard until 8:00 P.M. Then Vito and I went for dinner. I went to the motel after dinner and watched TV. Lonely.

MARCH 7
Left W.B. at 4:45. Got home and drank. Syl came after her date. We argued.

MARCH 8
Was drinking when Syl awoke. Had violent argument. She left. Ann and Danny came for dinner. Sooooooo drunk. And lonely.

MARCH 9
Spent whole day alone, recovering. Was to have gone to Mother and Dad's but couldn't make it.

MARCH 10
Left for W.B. at 6:00 A.M. Worked with Bob and Vito. We all went to dinner. Then I went to motel and studied for class at Lehigh. Everything in my life is wrong.

MARCH 11
Left W.B. at 4:30. Fed the dog and finished my case study for class presentation. It went well. Got home from Lehigh University at 10:00 P.M. Very tired. This is such a lousy schedule and it doesn't help to get home to an empty house. If only I'd meet someone who I could really love. They're either too old, too young, or too stupid. Want someone my age, attractive, *intelligent* with a sense of humor, compassionate and loves dogs. What's so hard about that?

MARCH 12
Went to Stratford. Got home and cleaned. Did errands. Had not wanted to drink, but did. Got very drunk. Called everyone I knew and some that I didn't. Spent money like it was going out of style. Feel very rebellious. Want to tell

the whole damn world to go jump off. Thought about that movie, *Stop the World, I Want to Get Off*. That's it precisely!

MARCH 13

Felt awful. Recovered on way to W.B. Drive seemed endless. Vito and I went for drinks after dinner, until 2:00 A.M. Got to motel, exhausted.

MARCH 14

Bad day. Got to office half hour late and Vito was already working. Had a tiff with Andy. Didn't give a damn about much.

MARCH 23

Spent entire day around the house, cleaning and doing errands. Took Mother and Dad for a ride but he got so tired he fell asleep. Very sad to watch. Was very happy to get home and away from them. Raked more leaves. Invited Syl to dinner but she had a date. A most beautiful day. Everything in bud. At 8:00 P.M., Ann called. She was upset. Wanted to talk. She came and we got drunk. My beautiful weekend shot.

MARCH 27

The last couple days like a nightmare. Managed to get to Wilkes-Barre but drunk most of the time. Ann invited me to a faculty party on Sunday.

It was another lovely Saturday but I awoke with a splitting headache and a bitter taste in my mouth. Disgust with myself possessed me. I didn't want to go to the faculty party Ann was having because I knew I would drink too much but I had promised I would help her prepare for it today. She was having twenty in for cocktails and dinner. Most of them I already knew and liked individually but, in a group, I'd always found academics dismal. All seemed to try too hard to be social when, in fact, most were really solitary persons who were comfortable with themselves alone but were painfully deficient in a social setting where small talk has a place.

With a great sigh, I got out of bed, holding my head with both hands. The bathroom seemed a thousand miles away but I managed to get to it and splashed water over my face, then put my head under the faucet in the bathtub. Gradually I began to be able to think. It was 10:00 A.M. I was to be at Ann's apartment as soon as I could get there.

I threw on some old slacks and grabbed a dress, slip, and shoes for tomorrow. What else would I need? Shoes for today. Bending over to get them sent a hundred pains shooting through my head. Brother, why do I always manage to do it? I asked myself.

With my clothing thrown over my arm, I went to the kitchen to look for recovery medicine. There was part of a bottle left standing on the kitchen cabinet. How had that happened? I wondered. Getting sensible, I guess, not finishing everything in sight? But then I remember that I had taken another bottle to bed with me! Ah yes, the great mystery solved. How glad I was to see something to drink. My head was like a hammer factory. Unsteadily I poured the remainder of the bottle into a glass. Just about four ounces. That should do it for now. In one gesture, I tossed off the whole quantity and waited for the effect. Ah, wonderful, that great rushing of warmth and surge. I felt like a new woman.

With a brisk step and energy, I grabbed my car keys and closed the doors behind me. It was a beautiful day. I had a small pang about not being able to stay home to work in the yard but I was now getting excited about the party. Two days of business and people, work and conversation. What could be better?

I savored the fifteen-mile drive to Bethlehem. It was a lovely time of year. For a few minutes, I felt very close to God, the Creator of everything my eyes could behold. Spring was in the air and the world was coming alive to a new season. Everything was just going so well for me. My classwork was good and I knew I could manage A's in both courses. Nothing to it. And my job . . . well, it paid well, what more need be said. It really wasn't so bad. And I liked working with Vito and Bob and sometimes Nick. And my new car, a station wagon, was just great, perfect for all the driving I was doing, which I really liked when I didn't have a hangover. And I had my farm, and a dog, and both parents. Life was certainly good to me. I had it all. Soon I'd be able to make the shift into college administration. Finishing my dissertation would help that, along with the work I was taking at Lehigh. Then I'd have my doctorate and six hours post-doctorate. And I was beginning to manage my dissertation. It was coming alive once again, and I was writing.

It was nice to feel so pleased with myself. Ah, what a beautiful day! Joy flooded through me.

I pressed the accelerator and made Ann's apartment in just minutes. As I locked the car, I gave it a long look as I walked away. It was a beautiful heavy new station wagon, the first I had ever owned. Soon it would be paid for. Soon.

As I went to press Ann's apartment bell, the door opened and she greeted me. I could see she had been drinking. Hope we get all the work done, I thought. Many times before she had passed out and I was left to finish the cooking. It had been like this much of the time we had known each other, having met our last year in college eighteen years earlier. From the very beginning we hit it off, probably because we both liked to drink. Ann was then engaged to a football player who was always trying to stay in training so we began going out for cocktails while Jack observed his rigid discipline. That camaraderie had led to our going to California after graduation and then to take our master's degrees together at Lehigh.

"I thought you might have forgotten," she said as she held the door wide for me.

"No, just slept too long."

We walked to the small apartment kitchen together.

"I've saved all the peeling and chopping for you." While she was talking, she was pouring rye into a glass. "Do you want soda?"

"I'll put it in."

Taking the bottle from her, I poured a small amount into the rye. I could taste the drink before drinking it. Again I was getting jittery and my head was splitting.

41

"Will you peel these onions? Have your drink first."

"Good idea."

I drank most of it in a few minutes. Never had to play games with Ann. She knew I was suffering. Never had to talk about it either. One or the other of us was usually suffering, sometimes both of us. We had many escapades together, escapades involving drinking that took place in about thirty of the fifty states. Maybe more than thirty. From the night before college graduation, when we had to be helped into a hotel room across the street from college because neither of us could drive . . . couldn't walk, as a matter of fact . . . to having to stay in some forlorn place in the Arizona desert because of not being able to function, we could gather unpleasant memories. Strangely enough, we found these episodes hilarious and frequently regaled others with them. Or the time we were in my car on the way to a place to drink and I drove into the back of a truck at a stoplight because I couldn't focus? Or the time I lost my college term paper while riding on the top of the back seat of the convertible with the top down?

Our "fun" ran into a generation of years. We represented the professional woman finishing advanced graduate work in dissertational exercise of intellectuality. And now we were about to entertain others of the same academic achievement. It was heady stuff.

The hours slipped by as we worked with industry brought about by a deadline. By early evening we had yet to do most of the cooking, for the day was spent in food preparation and silver polishing. Our entertaining together also went back many years. We worked well together in a kitchen. None of our habits annoyed the other and often we worked silently, just being at peace with leisurely drinking and pleasant occupation. I had begun to feel very drunk, a heavy kind of drunk, one that I couldn't shrug off. I hated this type. Sometimes I just couldn't overcome the effects of the liquor. It stayed with me and this was one of those times. Several times I soaked my head in cold water so I could drink more but it didn't help to revive me. Ann must have put me to bed sometime during the evening because I awoke and couldn't get adjusted to time and place, but after a struggle of monumental proportion, I discovered I was in the bedroom of her apartment and the clock read 5:00 A.M.

I stumbled into the hallway and then to the kitchen, where Ann was already working. I was very drunk. It was as if I hadn't slept at all. My eyes refused to focus. I hated myself.

"Hi. How are you feeling?" she asked perfunctorily.

"O.K. I guess. When did you get up?"

"Around three. Here, help yourself." She handed me a bottle. I noticed that I had finished a fifth the day before. I was sick, sick, sick, I felt and looked green. And yellow.

"I think I'd better go home before the party," I mumbled.

"You'll be all right. Just go back to bed for a while."

"But I want to help. That's what I came for," I said.

"Go to bed. I can finish it. You did everything."

I had a drink and went back to the bedroom but I was hurriedly moved to the bathroom and was ill. Retching, choking, feeling like my stomach was never going to be where it should be. I sat on the bathroom floor and held my head. You big jerk! What was I going to do? I couldn't get home, I couldn't stay in bed during the party, and I couldn't seem to stop the retching to get to the kitchen for a drink. Oh God, help me, help me! Get me out of this maze. . . .

You damn big jerk, Jean. Get yourself off the floor and tough it out. You're *not* sick, not sick, not sick. Manage your mind and get off the self-pity . . . that's it, now sit up slowly, get up s-l-o-w-l-y. . . . There. See. You can do it.

Straightening up, I gently threw water on my face. Then I used toothpaste and scrubbed my mouth with a washcloth, covering the inside of my cheeks and gums and tongue. There, that certainly tastes better. Now look for Alka-Seltzer. There. Just get some booze for it and you'll be a new woman.

Taking the Alka-Seltzer to the kitchen, I knew that I could make the party but it would be a touch-and-go matter and I'd have to be very careful.

"Thought you'd gone back to bed?" Ann stated.

"Decided I want to help. This Alka-Seltzer should do it."

"It will certainly do something," she said with disdain. "How can you drink that stuff?"

"It really works. But I always put a shot in it and then it doesn't taste so bad."

I did that and managed to get it down rather successfully. I held my breath momentarily, not knowing if it was safe to stay in one spot and breathe.

But I was O.K. Just very woozy and very hung over. My thoughts were muddled and my eyes were not focusing very well.

Our working hours were repeated and by afternoon I again felt terrific. The guests were beginning to arrive and I was able to mingle with them although I knew I couldn't move too quickly. Occasionally I staggered and I had some trouble with conversations. I knew I was again very drunk but I was sure no one noticed.

And then it was over and I didn't know where the time had gone. Again I found myself on the bed but heard voices in the distance. They were talking about me, I was sure of that. Talking about the fool I had made of myself. Well, I'd fix that!

I half fell off the bed. Oh, Jean, why, why, why, why, why do you do this? Go home and never go away again. Oh, to be home and alone and away from all these damn stupid people. I hate them. I hate everyone. I hate Ann. I hate myself.

I *must* get home. Why don't they stop talking about me? I fell toward the doorway and into the hallway. "Stop talking about me," I screamed at Ann and Tom and someone else whom I didn't know or didn't recognize. "Shut up, shut up!"

Two startled faces looked at me as I struggled to hold myself to the doorframe.

Ann came to me and began to lead me away. "Get back to bed."

"No, I'm going." I jerked my arm away from her. She was also drunk and staggered back into the room.

"Then go."

Tom rose. "Don't go. You can't drive."

Ann said, "Let her go. That's what she wants to do. When she gets like this, no one can do anything."

44

Tom still tried to hold me back but I pushed him away. Somehow I found my car keys. I was still fully clothed so I pushed my way out of the apartment, stumbling and lurching down the three flights of stairs, hitting the banister and stopping every few seconds.

Finally I was in the fresh air. It was heaven. I took great gulps of it. Oh, I was so eager to get to my home to go to bed and recover.

After fumbling a few moments for the right car key, I found it and got the door opened. It was hard to get behind the wheel but I finally did. Oh, to be home . . .

Starting the car, I foggily knew I had to be careful. My reflexes weren't so swift. Clumsily I put the car into drive and moved away from the curb. The wagon was a heavy and big car. It seemed to be leading me away from the curb. It was pulling me. I was very aware of the power and the easy handling. Trying to get around the corner too quickly, the front wheel went over the curb but bounced right back into the street as I swerved. The front end bounced hard. I was momentarily scared.

Damn it, Jean, be careful. You've got to get out of Bethlehem and get home. Just fifteen miles.

The streets confused me and I seemed to be lost. Finally I recognized the college campus. When I looked back to the street, there was a red light. I couldn't get the car stopped, my foot missed the pedal.

CRASH!

Oh damn. I cringed inside myself. I wanted to fall into nowhere. Then a man was at the window of my car, yelling at me.

"What the hell's the matter with you? You drove right into me. Ain't you got brakes on this heap of junk?"

"Why don't you just drop dead?" I screamed right back. Rage filled me.

I began to shake and perspire. I fumbled into my handbag and tried to find a card with my insurance number. Other cars were blowing horns for us to move and his wife came to my car, urging him to forget it.

"My name is Jean Kirkpatrick, Quakertown. Allstate insurance."

His wife pulled him away. He was still screaming and waving a fist.

I just wanted to get away. As best I could, I pulled my car around theirs and fed gas. My station wagon again pulled me. The power was enormous and I couldn't manage. Suddenly I was in an intersection and collided hard with another car. The noise was heavy. Glass shattered and metal twisted. My car was a mess, the entire front pushed in. The wagon was pushed up over a sidewalk and had narrowly missed a telephone pole. Then it came to rest, far away from the car I'd hit.

My heart was thudding. I had to get away but I knew I had to talk to the people. As best I could, with a superhuman effort, I got out of my station wagon and got to their car. It was a young man and a woman, who might be his mother.

"Are you hurt?"

"No."

I hurried back to the car.

Please, God, get me back to my car and away from here. Please, God, help me to get home. I'll never drink again, never.

I was almost paralyzed with fear. I was icy cold. I knew I was probably in shock when my teeth chattered and I was shaking. But I had to leave.

The car moved but it seemed no longer to have power. The entire hood was pushed back to the windshield. But I made every effort to get away before the police arrived and I got away as fast as I could.

Be careful, Jean. Don't hit anything. Don't let anyone see you. Move on out. Get away.

It may have been hours or half hours or minutes, but I managed to get back to Ann's apartment. I felt relief. She would help me.

I rang the bell and when Ann answered I could see that I had made a mistake. Her look told me how disgusting I appeared. It always struck me as being strange. We could drink together and get very smashed but she always showed utter disgust for me, probably because I became hyperactive and she passed out as a rule.

"I need help. *Please* help me. Take me home."

Suddenly she seemed very sober. "I can't. Tom's here. Go to bed."

"I'm going home. I've had it. I'm sick. Won't you both drive me home?"

It was daylight and Sylvia called me to the phone. I mumbled a "Hello."

"Mrs. Kirkpatrick? This is the Bethlehem police."

I was totally confused. Who the hell was this? What was he saying?

"Are you there, Mrs. Kirkpatrick?"

"What do you want?" bluntly I asked, annoyed and angry.

"This is the police. Do you know where you left your car?"

For a moment I was stunned. Where I left my car? Nasty, jagged pieces of memory tried to rip into my conscious mind. I heard the crash of metal and a picture of the twisted steel of the car hood poked through my twisted brain mass.

"Just a minute." I put the phone down and, icy with fear, I ran to the window that looked out onto the driveway. There was no car there except for Sylvia's.

I shook Sylvia, who had fallen asleep again. "Sylvia, Sylvia." My voice was hysterical. "Sylvia, where's my car?"

"It's at Ann's. Remember?"

I hadn't, but now I began to. Oh, God, what happened? Did I hit anyone? If only I could remember. If only . . .

I felt dazed. And very frightened. Maybe I'd have to kill myself to get out of this scrape. It was all up, the whole messy business of my life. For a split second, I felt relief at having decided simply to end it all, not be responsible for the mess I created.

I moved back to the phone.

"My car is in Bethlehem." I paused before mustering my

most controlled and "in charge" voice. "I'm sorry I have been so long in answering. Morning was never my best time. Can I tell you something about the accident?" I was all sugar and cooperation. But I was really shaking inside.

"You are charged with hit-and-run. When can you come in?"

Hit-and-run! Hit-and-run? *Hit-and-run!* Did I hit someone?

"I'll be right there. Where shall I come?"

"I'll meet you at your car in a half hour," he said briskly.

"I'll be right there," I said again. But where was my car?

Placing the phone back into its cradle, I collapsed into a chair, limp, shaking, perspiring. What have I done? I was unable to believe that this was reality. My mind was very foggy and I had a very major hangover. I had to have a drink but I was certain nothing was around. I was desperate. I had to find something so that I could meet the policeman. None of the liquor stores were open and no bar was yet open. What to do? There had to be something.

I tried not to awaken Sylvia for a minute or two. She was a heavy sleeper, especially after a day in the intensive care unit at the hospital.

Think, Jean. Think. There was no Listerine or cooking sherry, all drunk before. Then I thought I remembered something in the barn I had spied the other day and wanted to catalogue in my mind for an emergency. This was surely it.

Putting on slippers, I made my way down the stairs and out to the barn. It was early morning, light, and I was still frightened but my necessity went beyond my fear.

Opening a small door to an annex room of the barn, I found the can of Sterno. Hurriedly I went to the house, pried off the top, and, with an old white cloth, squeezed the beautiful purple Sterno through, filtering it to produce liquid.

There was only a small quantity, but I knew it would do the trick for now. I found some soda and put a generous amount with it. It was a beautiful drink and it ended the immediate shakes that had been with me from the moment of the phone call, some twenty minutes before.

Now to get Sylvia, but first I had to get rid of the evidence of my drink. I stuffed the can and lid into a trash bag and buried the now stained purple cloth at the bottom of it.

What was I going to do? What had happened? Should I go to Bethlehem or should I just go take the pills? Better wait until you have a bottle to do that. Can't face that in the real light of sobriety.

God, won't you help me? Imploringly I raised a hand. Then I was angry and shook my fist skyward. "Why did You let me down?" Everyone let me down. No one ever helped me. No one. Ever. By damn, I'll show those jerks. Real jerks, that's what they all are. Who the hell do they think they are? Who?

But my anger and bravado and rage dissolved into fear again. I was really scared, almost to death but not close enough. If only I could die. "God, why don't You strike me dead? Go ahead. See if I care."

Then I thought it might really happen. "I'm sorry, God, I didn't mean it, honest I didn't."

You coward, you big dumb pleading frightened weak-kneed coward. You jerk. You stupid ass, you crud.

What was I going to do? I *had* to go to Bethlehem and face the police. What had really happened? I couldn't think about it.

Slowly I went to get Sylvia. I shook her awake and told her where we had to go.

"I think you should go alone," she said sleepily.

"But I can't!"

"Why not? I think it will look better."

Brother, I wasn't ready for that jolt.

"Won't you please go?" I implored.

"No," she said flatly.

I knew it was impossible to deal with her when she said *no* like that.

Sighing heavily and with resignation, I quickly dressed, almost oblivious to my pounding head, shaking hands, nausea. Fear and trepidation overcame those for these moments. I dressed in a two-piece suit and wore heels so that I'd look like a businesswoman who had simply made a mistake.

While I dressed I planned how to get a bottle. I knew a

place to stop on the way to Bethlehem and I knew I could recover before seeing the police. But I had to take parsley and mouthwash with me and spray perfume.

Finally together, and with the promising thought of a bottle, I got Sylvia's car keys and headed out to her car.

It was just past 8:00 A.M. and a glorious day but I hardly noticed it, I was so immersed in my troubles.

I started the car and got out of the driveway in a cloud of dust. Had to get that bottle fast.

Ten minutes later I had it, having stopped at a place in Hellertown on the way to Bethlehem. Oh, the ambrosia. *Now* I knew that everything could be managed. No matter what had happened, I was sure it would be solvable. I'd just simply say I was sorry for whatever I did and then repair it. I'd snowed others before with seeming ignorance, or innocence, or "I'm-just-not-able-to-understand-what-I-did" routine, or "Poor-little-me-needs-your-brains-and-help" routine. I always felt comfortable in knowing I could make up a usable routine for every occasion. Slick intelligence. Or necessity? Or hot air? Or cunning? Or a cheap shot at dummies?

Recovering now, I began to think about where I was going. I'd go first to Ann's in the hope the car was there. Syl had said it was but I couldn't remember. Had Ann seen the car? Brother, I hope she had. All her fault. Well, not *all* her fault but if it hadn't been for that stupid business in her apartment, I wouldn't have been driving and had the accident.

Rounding the corner of Stefco Boulevard, I soon was at her apartment house and there was my car, all smashed up and the two right wheels on the sidewalk. And there were the police. Two of them, waiting.

I munched parsley and sprayed some cologne around my head. I had to act normal but I was really very hung over. It was an end-of-the-world feeling again. Oh, why did I do it? I'm going to quit. Never again will I touch a drop. Never! I can't go through this stuff anymore. It just seems like I can't drink anymore. Maybe those years in AA were right. At least I didn't get into trouble all the time. And I never had hangovers.

I parked Syl's car and got out easily.

"Good morning," I said cheerily. "What's this about a hit-and-run charge?" I asked, taking the offensive, commonly known as taking the bull by the horns. In this case, taking the fuzz by surprise.

They walked over to me.

"Are you Mrs. Jean Kirkpatrick?"

"Yes."

"Were you in an accident yesterday with this car?"

"Yes."

"Why did you not report the accident?"

"Because I didn't know it needed reporting."

"Why didn't you stay at the scene of the accident?"

"Because I didn't know I should stay. I went to the people in the car and asked if anyone was hurt. They said no. And so I left."

Then he gave me a long lecture on procedures and methods of the law. Meanwhile the other officer was scrutinizing me carefully. They looked like they would accept a reasonable story so I began explaining about the company I worked for, that I had been to a party, that I didn't know Bethlehem, that the accident scared me badly, that I went home and was very upset, that I hadn't called because they would think it ridiculous that I didn't know where the accident happened.

With enough talking and with a show of my cards of identification and for whom and where I worked and that I was under great stress, blah, blah, blah, I was let go.

"There will be a hearing for which you will be notified where and the time. Then you will be heard for the charge of hit-and-run."

"May I please have a copy of the accident report?"

"Here."

"You see, when the people weren't hurt, I didn't take their names." I paused. "I guess that's what I should have done that I didn't."

"Ma'am, there was everything you should have done that you didn't," he said dryly.

Then they gave me the names of the persons whose car I hit and the name of the street where it happened.

"Did you want any more information?" I asked co-operatively.

"Not just now. But, hereafter, know the law and follow it. This time you were very lucky."

"Yes, I will do that. And I appreciate your help and concern."

They touched the brims of their hat rims with a finger in a little salute.

I watched them get into the squad car. Perspiration was running down the length of my body. All my clothes were soaking wet. I could feel myself starting to shiver and I knew the nausea was about to begin.

I gave a little wave of my hand and walked over to my station wagon. It was a mess of twisted steel. My beautiful wagon. I tried to open a front door but couldn't so I opened a back door and felt under the seat. No bottle. Thank God. All the time we were talking I wondered if any bottles were in the car. Guess not.

Now I had to get home and try to see what I could do about this mess. What if I lost my license? What if the people I hit would sue?

I got into Syl's car and took a long drink, not caring who saw me. The need was greater than pride.

Driving home, I realized it was Monday and I hadn't even thought of work or my job. Guess I'd better call Nick. Maybe I'd get fired for this, just another inexcusable lapse. So, what the hell? Who cares? I'd like to chuck the whole bit. Everything. Just get in my car and go. Well, guess I can't do even that. Must wait until it is fixed. But then I will. Pack up, sell everything, and just drive off into the sunset. Why not? There surely wasn't anything to stop me.

When I got back to Quakertown I went right to the liquor store. Better stock up, since Sylvia will be leaving with her car and I'll be stuck. What in the hell will I do? Another problem!

After getting the liquor, I put it into the barn so Syl wouldn't know about it. Then I went into the house.

"Hi, what happened?"

I told her everything. "Now I've got to get Walter on the phone." He was my insurance agent.

"He'll help you. But what's going to happen?"

"I don't know. There will be a hearing in a few weeks. But you should see my car. It's bad."

"You don't seem nearly as concerned as you were. Is everything O.K.? Ah, I see, you've been drinking."

She had walked within range of my breathing.

"Well, I guess nothing is wrong with the world now, right?" She looked sadly at me and shook her head. "When are you going to get with it? You have so much in every way. Why do you do this to yourself? I can't stand seeing it."

In a rare moment of honesty, I said, "I don't know why. I really want to stop. I try. Every day I think it will be different but then I have to recover. I don't want to be this way."

I was sobbing quietly.

"Call someone. Go back to AA. You've got to have help. You know you can't do it alone. But just do it. Each time the trouble gets worse."

"I know. I know."

"I've got to go to work," Syl said and then left. She embraced me before leaving and I could see how very upset she was. I wanted to explain that it just happened. I wanted to tell her it wouldn't happen again, but I couldn't promise that. I wanted to say how sorry I was for all the trouble I brought her and I wanted to say thanks for everything and I wanted to cry and promise that tomorrow everything would be different and I wanted to apologize for being so weak, so without character, so without strength.

Instead I mustered bravado and gave her a big reassuring smile. "Everything will be O.K. And thanks for helping me."

I walked to the car with her.

"Be good," she said, just before driving out the lane.

I watched the taillights of her car as she put on the brakes before pulling out into the road. I hated to see her go. As long as she was around, my situation didn't seem to be so frightening, but now, alone, the seriousness of it gripped me.

I walked to the barn and got the bottles I had put there. I

went into the house in a rush, hoping no one would see me, even though that was highly unlikely.

In the house I poured myself a drink but left it on the sink counter. I hated it and what it was doing to me. For a long moment I looked at it analytically and wondered how I could have become so dependent upon this. Quickly, I turned away and began to walk through the rooms of the house. It was again distorted. Nothing seemed to be right. The house felt wrong and every room seemed different from anything I knew. I felt strange and alienated from reality.

In the living room I sat in a chair and just sort of stared into nowhere. My mind just refused to think about the shambles of my life. Still I had not called Nick to say why I was not coming to work. Nor had I called the insurance agent. It seemed that my life these days was just a matter of trying to keep up with the problems that my drinking created. I had to stop. I just had to give up ever drinking again. Somehow I had deluded myself into believing I could handle it, yet eleven years had flown by since that day when I received the telegram about the fellowship for my dissertational work. Still not done. Would it ever be? My company had given me all the time in the world to be away from the office to do it. I had been home six months with a broken foot and hadn't finished it, just played with it. Now more trouble. The volcano of dissatisfaction inside of me seemed to be rumbling trouble. I wanted to run, to jump, to scream, to beat my fists against a wall, to bang my head, to punch everything in sight. Now, without a car, I felt more trapped than ever before.

What did I have to do to get my life back into order? When was it I last had order in it? Eleven years before, when I was at the University of Pennsylvania and wasn't drinking. But how could I do that now? Order was impossible. My dissertation was unfinished. My job would soon be terminated. My life had no direction, since who would hire me at forty-five? And money, what would I do for it? I needed my final degree to get a job at forty-five and I couldn't get that degree until I finished my dissertation, which I knew I couldn't do. Just thinking about it made me break out into perspiration. Why are you so afraid of failure? Why? Other people fail and it doesn't throw them. Why are you so damned special? Who the hell do you think you are?

The feeling of being trapped in the house and into a life that I didn't want or like sent me flying to the kitchen for the drink I left standing on the counter top.

Damn, damn, damn, damn, damn. I reached for the drink and just threw it into my mouth. I had to swallow quickly to keep from choking. Some of it spilled over the front of my sweater. I looked down at it and saw the messiness. Now I was really a lush, booze all over the front of my clothes.

Aw nuts. I began to feel sorry for myself so I poured another real heavy drink and put just a splash of soda into it. No ice, thank you. It spoils the effect. I also drank it hurriedly. This time my eyes watered and I spluttered as the harsh liquor scratched past my throat. Ah, that's more like it. Self-inflicted pain.

Probably an hour slipped by before I called Nick, who was upset by my absence. But I placated him by saying I would borrow or rent a car tomorrow.

Then I called Walter, who was both a friend and insurance agent. When I told him everything he was aghast and told me that it was quite serious.

"But you'll get me out of it, won't you?"

"I'll do what I can to learn what has happened. Where did it happen?"

"Just a minute, I'll look. It's on the report."

"Don't you know?" he asked incredulously.

"No, I don't remember."

"That's a hell of a note." He was angry.

Looking at the report, I told him the streets but couldn't tell him anything more.

"Send me the report. And I'll get back to you as soon as I know anything more. You know, you better go easy on the stuff. This is real bad news, Jean."

"Gosh, Walter, I know that. I've already decided to quit."

"I'm very glad to hear that. I sure hope it's in time."

Well, how do you like that? Now my insurance agent tells

me when to quit. Brother, that did it. So I poured another very heavy drink and wondered what to do with the day. Maybe I'll work on my dissertation. Not bad thinking. And maybe I'll do the paper for Lehigh. Get some order, that's the name of the game. Discipline. Self-discipline. Character. Maturity. Better get another nice drink before getting out all the dissertation notes and papers. It was really beginning to taste good and I felt like I could finish my dissertation today. Maybe in a day or two. But soon. That was the key to my future.

As I carried my drink to the living room I suddenly remembered that I had no automobile. The trapped feeling came back. I had to call the garage that had picked up the car and hurry them into finishing the work.

Dialing the number for the garage was difficult. It struck me that my drinks were hitting me and it was only 10:00 A.M. So what? Who the hell cares? The world is out there, going on. I'm trapped in here, sealed into my own tomb, one of my own making. I could break out if I wanted to, but why? What for? Who would miss me?

I stopped trying to dial. I no longer cared when the car would be finished. It really made no difference. I never wanted to go anywhere ever again. The hell with the whole world.

I lurched to the kitchen and took the bottle with me, leaving the glass on the counter top where the bottle had been.

I threw myself into a chair in front of the TV and drank as I thought about it. Sometime later the bottle fell away from me and I slept. Not until the middle of the night did I awaken and feel great panic, not knowing where I was, a white TV screen the only light in the room. My skin was crawling and I felt my stomach beginning to heave. Again and again the nausea rolled over me. I tried to rise in an effort to get to the kitchen to get more liquor but couldn't push myself out of the chair, because I was still too drunk to get my brain to make my body move.

Groaning, cursing, crying, retching, I let myself fall back into the chair. Perspiration poured out of me and I wanted to die. Why couldn't I just die? Why? Again the nausea covered me in waves of waterish brash filling my mouth. Swallowing hard, I tried to keep it from spilling out of my mouth. I had to get a drink. Falling out of the chair, I began to crawl to the kitchen. Just like a damn dog but not even as maneuverable, I thought. Anyone here to pet me, love me, care if I stay in or go out?

In the kitchen doorway, I pulled myself up to reach the counter and the supply I had bought yesterday. Yesterday? When? Was it yesterday? Ah, who cares what day. Just recover because today I know I am going to quit. No more feeling disgust, no more sickness, no more fear or rage or humiliation or loneliness or up-chucking. It's worth it just to be rid of the up-chucking. But first the recovery drink to stop the upheaval of my stomach. My hand caught a new bottle and I wrestled with the seal. Damn thing! *Why* do they have to seal them? The bottle slipped from my grasp onto the kitchen floor. I was startled and let out a cry of surprise and anger. But it hadn't broken. Good thing they use heavy glass, that's what I thought.

Moments later I ripped off the seal and took a long, long drink. Immediately I had problems with it staying where I put it. Hanging my head over the sink, I waited long enough to try again. And again. By the third try I was able to feel that it would remain in my stomach long enough for the effect of the alcohol to take place.

A long sigh escaped me. At last I could manage. With caution now, I took small sips. Didn't want to get drunk today because I was going to quit today, forever and ever and ever. That's one long period of time, Jean. Well, maybe I'll quit for a week. That's much better. But first I've got to recover.

Leaning on the sink counter, I looked out the kitchen windows. Looked like just past dawn. But what day? What month? What had happened?

My mind just couldn't seem to put events into place. There was the accident. Oh, why did you think about that now! Take a drink and get back to the TV. There will be enough to worry about later but, right now, get yourself together.

I seemed to be feeling pretty good. I was able to walk back into the living room. Something was on TV now. An agricultural report of some kind. Not very interesting but something to focus on. I worked hard at keeping my attention centered on the picture and the words. Sometimes I got one, sometimes another, but my mind refused to synchronize the two. So what else is new?

My mind seemed exceptionally befuddled. I shook my head hard. That did it. A groan formed and I expressed it. Just get through this day so you can quit. Quit. Heaven. I just want peace and good health. No more being scared.

The "Today" show came on TV and I was able to get absorbed in it. After that the game shows started and I watched those, telling myself I was recovering, but I noticed the liquor was disappearing. Well, when it was all gone I'd have to quit. That's how I'd quit. No one to get me liquor.

Sometime during early evening I awoke. Scared and frightened. Teeth chattering. Cold. Hungry. Where was I? Home, this is home.

The TV had Dr. Welby. It was comforting to identify what was on the TV screen. I felt some security. Good old Dr. Welby, friend of the family. Any family but not my family.

Damn nausea is starting, Jean. Get a drink. Hurry. Hurry. Geez, I couldn't get out of the chair again. Moving to the side, I slipped out of the chair and fell to the floor. Ah nuts. Get up, you damn fool. But I couldn't get up. I felt a thousand years old and tired. So damn tired. The predictable retching began. The bitter liquid ran out of my mouth and I began choking. Spasms went over me and, then, I was trying to get breath while swearing to myself. You big, damn, stupid, utter, disgusting thing. You're an animal. You pig. You loathsome piece of humanity that's not even human.

Save it, Jean. Not now. Just recover. By some strange quirk, I found a bottle on the floor in front of the TV with a half pint in it. Thank you, God. Thank you.

I drank it as best I could. But it refused its new home. My clothes were soaked. Had to get to the bathroom, but how? Crawl, just crawl. That's where you belong, on the ground, crawling.

Crawling, on all fours, falling in a heap on the floor, crawling again, sobbing and cursing, I got to the bathroom with a great burst of effort after a seeming eternity of five or ten minutes. I struggled to get out of my clothes, which took another superhuman burst of effort. Panic gripped me. I got stuck half in and half out of my sweater. My heart thumped and I felt sick, trapped, strangled, unable to breathe. Lashing out my arms in a wild, hysterical fashion, I ripped the sweater and was finally free. Free? Free? You stupid, idiotic, imbecilic fool.

I laid my head on the floor and I was in a twisted heap, but it made no difference whatever. I wanted to die. Just die. The nausea began again. This time I laid my head on the edge of the toilet seat. Maybe I'd have to spend the rest of my unnatural life there if I couldn't stop the bitter, heavy white fluid that kept filling my mouth. Oops, this time it was green, a sickly, smelly green.

Then the spell was over and I again crumpled on the floor, exhausted. I slept for a few hours and then awoke to the stench and mess of my clothes and the last episode of retching.

At last I was able to get out of the remaining clothes I had on. I felt much better than I had earlier. My stomach was empty and I seemed almost sober. Almost real. I pulled myself up by holding on to the bathtub and found that I could stand, although my head was broken in several places, or so it felt.

I managed to run the water for the bathtub but didn't wait for it to fill but took a washcloth and soap and lathered my whole body while standing beside the tub. Oh, it felt sooo good. And smelled so good. I felt almost jubilant. Almost.

There was even a bottle under the tub, partially visible at one tub leg. As I reached down to get it, I slipped and fell against the tub. Looking to see where I cut myself, I saw many bruises all over my body. Where had they come from? Where was I?

No matter. I opened the bottle and took a long, pleasant drink. Ah, that wonderful warmth that flooded my body, radiating from my stomach. Terrific.

Today was the magic day to quit. Hurriedly I washed off the soap and dried myself. Gee, I really felt terrific. Maybe I'd eat. I felt ravenously hungry.

Getting to the kitchen was no real problem, although I was staggering badly. I had no sense of balance but I did manage to get there in an upright position, walking, with the supportive aid from the side walls.

The kitchen was a mess but I didn't remember what from. Ah well, no matter. But I had trouble finding some clean dishes. An inspection of the cupboards showed little to eat and nothing I was hungry for, so I called a restaurant in town and asked if they would deliver several platters because I was caring for some elderly people. Yes, in this case, they would. So I ordered two roast beef dinners and several dishes of jello.

While I waited for the food to come, I tried to reconstruct the past few days. Or was it weeks? Lately I seemed to lose whole sections of time. Where did they go? Was I losing my mind? Why couldn't I remember?

I began to wonder how I could know. Ask the operator. Why not? Lifting the phone receiver, I dialed "O" and then asked, "What is the date, please?" She told me. "What is the day?" Her voice sounded peculiar when she answered that it was Tuesday. Tuesday?

Neither the day nor the date meant anything. Baloney, have a drink. But was there anything? I looked through all the cupboards. There was an empty Sterno can. When did I drink that? In a moment I found a half pint. That was it. Why didn't I have my car? I *had* to get it. Can't go on like this.

I opened the half pint and the smell made me ill. Quickly I closed it and admired myself for my attitude. There, Jean, it's not so hard to give up drinking. It smells terrible and you never ever want to drink again. Hate it. Look at the mess it made for me. At last, I'll quit.

A knock on the door and there was food. The delivery person looked over my shoulder at the mess all over the kitchen. I acted like there was nothing unusual and paid him.

"Thanks."

Closing the door, I uncovered the food and ate as if I hadn't eaten for weeks. The food tasted wonderful. I ate everything at once, not bothering with the niceties.

I finished both plates of food and ate both dishes of jello. I was still hungry, so I ate some crackers and cheese I had. Then I found some tuna fish and opened it and ate. I topped it all off with some chocolate milk and pretzels. It all tasted like the finest of international cuisine.

I managed to get several hours' sleep before being awakened by the phone. It was Sylvia.

"How are you?"

"Great. I've stopped drinking. Had two platters of food. How's that?"

"Wonderful. I'm so glad to hear it. Do you remember my saying I couldn't come for the rest of the week? I have exams and floor duty."

I hadn't remembered a thing and I was very disappointed. What would I do for a car?

"Sure, I remember. When will I see you?"

"Early part of next week. Wish me luck, O.K.?"

"You've got it."

"When will you get your car?"

"I don't know, but I'll call today."

"Have you heard anything more about the hearing?"

The hearing? What hearing? My long silence prompted her to say:

"I'm sorry I brought it up. I guess you're still pretty shaken up from the accident. Anyway, let me know. I'll call over the weekend if I can."

Accident? *Accident?* Then I began to remember the accident. And everything. Being without my car had not been connected in my mind with the remembrance of any accident.

"Jean, do you hear me?"

"Oh, yes, what did you say?" I was completely lost in the conversation.

"I said that I probably won't be able to call but I'll try over the weekend. Take care."

"You bet. And thanks for calling. See you."

" 'Bye. Be good. And I'm so glad you're quitting."

She hung up while I stood rooted to the floor, looking stupidly at the telephone.

A shiver of fear ran over me. The accident. What had really happened? Was I supposed to call Walter? Did I call Walter? Had I hit someone?

I got the half pint opened again and this time I drank without caution or reserve. My aim was to get the courage to make several phone calls and to blot out any other memory.

And then I had to wrestle with the problem of getting something to drink. Panic was beginning to get to me. I dialed the taxi company and mentioned my problem. I knew the owner kept a bottle in the cab for people who needed to buy one in a hurry. I wondered how many other people in town used this service. I bet the driver could tell a tale of who the alcoholics are.

But he said he'd come and, ten minutes later, I had a fifth of Calvert at twice the price, but that made no difference whatever.

I began serious drinking right away but it didn't taste very good because I had eaten. And there was no quick reaction to the liquor, no nice warm feeling flowing through me. Just a bad taste in my mouth. I didn't even like it. It tasted horrible. I shuddered as I swallowed it but I knew if I kept at it, it would soon change. Maybe it would take a couple of hours but it would happen. All I had to do was put up with the bad taste now. Ugh! horrible stuff, this liquor. Why do I bother? I wondered while I drank and looked out on to the big field outside my kitchen window.

What's it all about anyway? Where am I going? Don't even go to see my parents because of not wanting them to see me this way. But they know. They sure do know! But they are busy with friends, always busy. Somehow we became a family disappointed in each other. There was so much about them that I didn't like. But, then, they didn't like me. Love me? I often wondered. They acted like they were supposed to love me. But I wondered if they did. Sometimes it taxed my mentality and emotions to find what I considered a shred of evidence. Where were they when I was in this or that? Or were they ever interested in my work or my achievements? Or me as a person? We never talked to each other. I was simply their DAUGHTER and was supposed to act the role. But I wasn't someone to know or to enjoy. I'd always been envious of my friends' relationships to their parents, who doted on their every word, their every action, their every achievement. So I went on collecting honors and medals and degrees, yelling, "Here I am, notice me." O.K., that's what my psychiatrist said. And it seemed true enough. I did want my parents to notice me and tell me I was worthy of their love, their esteem.

Jean, that's a real joke. Boozed up, drunk. Worthy of esteem. You big jerk!

I was again getting sick and very drunk. I had to get to a chair or to bed or somewhere. The feeling of being stuck in the house was beginning to get to me. I always did feel trapped, but without a car I was encased in my own tomb. That's the way the house seemed to me recently.

Sick, sick, sick, I began to sing at the top of my lungs. It was more like a singing scream I guess but it helped to relieve the tension. It felt as if my heart were bleeding, as if all of me were dying a slow bleeding death. How to get out? How really! Joke's on you, Jean. A big yak. You'll never get out alive, isn't that what *they* say? Oh, that's funny, real funny. Then why aren't you laughing? Before that, you'll have to straighten up and fly right. No more guilt, no more remorse. But why do I feel so damn guilty all the time? What the hell have I done except be a miserable excuse for a human being? Your parents, that's it, the way you treat them, or don't treat them, as the case may be. But, damn it, they hurt me too! But why can't I be kind, understanding, reasonable, be what they want me to be? Which is? Oh, to be married and have a family, to be like other people, to fade into the woodwork of normality, to be small-town molded and mellowed, to be like everyone else, never be controversial. Rats, I'd rather be dead. See, you dummy, that's the way this whole conversation began.

I turned on the radio and got the wildest music I could find. Then I turned up the volume to ear-splitting level and began to throw myself around in a dervish, to be rid of the wildness that was in me. Whirling made me very dizzy and I was unable to catch myself as I started to fall down the curving, tapered stairwell. Falling, falling, falling . . . It caught me by surprise. When I stopped falling, I landed in a ball at the foot of the stairwell. A few moments passed and then I began to inspect myself. Hmmmmm . . . nothing seemed broken, and it didn't even seem like me. Crazy again, just like twelve years ago when you were in a looney hospital. Not everyone can say that. Ah me . . . I was so tired I stayed lying in a heap at the foot of the stairs. My mind drifted away from my body and exhaustion and drunkenness overcame the mental gyrations.

When I awoke it was daylight and I didn't know where I was. Supreme confusion was all I knew. Damn, damn, damn, damn. I tried to arise but couldn't. My arm was twisted beneath me and was almost paralyzed. There was no circulation in it. My legs were twisted. Each small attempt to straighten out was painful. I groaned. Then I became aware of the radio blaring. It was suddenly all too much. I screamed at the top of my lungs, "Help. Hellp. Helllllp. Helllllllp. Won't someone please help me? Just hear me? Oh, please help me!" I wept in self-pity and shame and remorse and guilt and total dejection and rejection of the thing called Jean.

Sobbing, I tried to roll over. Gradually I began to get myself unwrapped but circulation to all extremities was very bad. My head was splitting, and I was beginning to retch. But I couldn't move. The sour fluid, the taste of something dead or dying. Yes, that's really it.

Since I couldn't arise, I tried to calm myself to stop the retching. I felt the bottle close by and tried to drink. It took long efforts and many but finally the retching was stopped and I sank back into oblivion.

Chapter 4

How many times have our families and friends called agencies to send someone to help us? But, of course, this never works, never brings about the desired result. It only evokes more resentment in us for their meddling in our affairs, affairs *we know* we can handle!

The decision to give up drinking must come from us, from the woman herself. It comes when a certain point of humiliation and sickness is reached. It comes when a point is reached from which one cannot go on for one more day. But many times before this final decision is reached, we have *wished* we could stop drinking. Unfortunately, it is when our hangovers are worse than usual. We really aren't *seriously* considering quitting at all, just quitting long enough to get over the day's hangover.

When I extracted the following last diary entries, I relived many of the terrible feelings I had when writing them so many years ago. How grateful I am for my life now! But you will know what I suffered, perhaps you are suffering the same now.

There are many pages across which is scrawled "DRUNK," sometimes in a way I could barely read.

"Spent morning on the couch. Tried recovering all day. By P.M. began to feel better. Only with God can I conquer all of my feelings of inadequacy and the need to drink. I MUST get some self-respect."

"Drunk all day. By P.M. had terrible distortion. There seemed to be someone in the house with me. Poured away the rest of the bottle. Sick, depressed, lonely."

"What a waste drinking is . . . what a waste!"

"Awoke and knew it would be a bad day. Wanted to stop drinking but decided I couldn't today. Very frightened."

"Drunk the whole damn day."

"Drunk. Called Help Line in N.Y.C. I am so lonely. Called them all through the night. Need desperately to live with someone but no one can stand me. Talked 2½ hours on the last call. Felt like killing myself." (Two months later I was hospitalized for attempted suicide.)

"Can't remember much about anything today."

"I must get a job! I must stop drinking."

"I hate myself. Need someone to talk to."

"Felt terrible all day. Was on couch and watched TV. Tapered off. Very frightened. Brought dog in."

"What is this madness? Why can't I stop? If I had something to live for . . ."

(Entry almost unreadable)
"Drunk as usual. Drunk when I awoke. Took Dexedrine. Called X and she wouldn't come. Didn't want to hear my troubles. Has too many of her own. Called Y and Z. They also wouldn't come. Looks like the end of the road. Must pull myself together. I got mad at God and blew up. Later I repented and was frightened. FACE YOURSELF AND THINK."

For all of us, there comes a day when family and friends do desert us, after having suffered as much as any people can endure, and then some. Finally those closest to us can no longer stand the hurt, can no longer forgive us, can no longer stay with us, for we have purposely driven them to the limits of human endurance.

Then we are alone, our world lying shattered about us, the world we broke into pieces. With our whipping boys gone, there is nothing to do but face ourselves, something we haven't done for a very long time.

But as we try to let up on drinking, try to taper off, the withdrawal that follows brings us fear known only to the alcoholic. So we drink again, more heavily than ever. Usually we land in a hospital, a gutter, or a police station. Sometimes we kill others in an auto accident.

But the end is at hand, the time for a decision, the time to face it is full upon us, once and for all.

My time of decision came after months of drinking and despair, months during which I did nothing other than drink and recover, only to drink again.

It may happen that way for you. Some morning when you awaken with a terrible hangover and are falling apart, ravished with remorse and disgust, guilt and depression, scrutinize yourself in a way you haven't done in years. Take a hand mirror and go to a window where sunlight is shining in, even though your hangover is so devastating you can't stand light. Now, look closely at your face. Notice the tiny broken blood vessels around the nose and in your cheeks, observe the deadness of your eyes, look at the dry and slaky quality of your skin and the uneven color of your face. See, too, the lines of tension. But, most especially, look at your whole face and comprehend the despair and unhappiness that is reflected. Have you ever seen an unhappier person?

Try to understand, and feel the full impact, that this sad, pitiable person is you. Know that you are sick as a result of drinking too long and too much.

Desire health, yearn to be rid of splitting headaches. Want to be rid of fright and self-disgust. Know that if others have managed to reverse this sickness, you can do so also. Know that you will no longer have to struggle to arise each morning, believing sometimes that death itself would be better. Remove thoughts of despair. Know that if you want to be well, it can be accomplished. Your family and friends stand willing to help you, but it is your decision to want that help that must come first.

This woman, you, must face not only the reality that a complete change must occur, but you must want that reality more than anything else in this world. This woman must know that alcohol has won, that the corner has been turned that reads "NEVER AGAIN."

In making a decision to quit, it helps to know that what you have is an incurable disease, one that will defeat you in every way. It will eventually destroy your life, if it hasn't already, it will blow your mind and forever ruin every relationship you have ever had. Did you know that every alcoholic affects, destroys, or disturbs the lives of five other people? Have you?

Does it help you to know that your decision to quit will, in time, reverse the pessimism and depression you have so long lived with? Try to imagine a new life with your family, a life in which you do not feel the restless inner urge that drives you in everything you do, even in drinking. Believe that you will have inner peace and calmness, happiness and acceptance, even respect from others. Think about the time to come when your family will no longer have to say "Mother isn't feeling well today" or any of the other countless excuses made by husbands, children, mothers, fathers, friends. Nor will you have to make the endless and empty excuses for not getting to work on time or not at all.

The decision to quit must spring from the despair or anger or disgust with self which must be accompanied by a deep and sincere desire to change, to remake life in a new mold. The decision must come from the realization and acceptance that your present way of living is futile and that a new way must be found. It is extremely important to know that you are not hopeless and that, with help, you can put this blight out of your life.

While drinking we are deceived into thinking that no one knows how much we drink. Or so I thought. When sober, however, I found that everyone knew but me. If you are like I was (and most of us tend to be generally alike in our thinking and drinking), you will be unbelieving, then embarrassed, at your not too well-kept secret being common knowledge.

During the first weeks of sobriety, I remember grocery clerks and minor acquaintances were friendlier and more concerned with me as an individual. It was not only because I was nicer when not drunk, but because they seemed to be genuinely happy that I had overcome a problem, the problem I didn't think anyone knew I had. The problem which, for so long, I would not be convinced I had.

Instances such as these will make your first days of sobriety happier because you will feel a respect for yourself that has been missing for a very long time. It will be reflected from others. Moreover, this new experience of friendliness makes maintenance of sobriety easier to endure because we feel pride when others express approval of us. But let me add a word of caution: do not be so overpleased with self that you feel it calls for a drink. This is a favorite self-deception of the alcoholic. This belief that now all is O.K. and a little harmless drink won't hurt.

Years of drinking narrow the personality without the drinker's awareness. We become subjective, egocentric, demanding, self-pitying, resentful. We are wrapped in a cocoon, aware only of self with no relation to others or the outside world. We weren't like this to begin with, but the insidiousness of alcohol's effects make us this way.

Whom do you consider daily other than yourself? Is anyone or anything in your mind besides alcohol and where to get it? Ask yourself when you last thought of other people . . . your mother, your father, husband, sister, brother, daughter, friends, neighbors? Do you know their problems? Have you concerned yourself with them?

If you are drinking, your answer will be that you haven't had time. If starting to dry out, now is the time to think of them. They could be a determining factor in your staying sober. By making yourself think about other people and their problems (and *everyone* has them, rich and poor), you will make the first step toward rejoining the world again. This part of sobriety is vastly important because, until you feel interest and compassion for others by overcoming your own self-pity, success over alcohol is doubtful.

During the period when I was trying to *control* my drinking, I was able to manage a day or two without alcohol. But then I would start drinking again and, once started, I had difficulty in stopping. That's when I asked myself why I drank on certain occasions and not on others. Why did I drink last Thursday but not the one before? What made all my high resolves disappear? Why was it that I didn't give a damn about anything, yet just the day before I was filled with happiness, firm resolve, and an exuberance from being sober?

Somehow it became clear to me that every time I felt wronged, slighted, put upon, I became defensive and self-pitying. Those were the times I ended up drinking. But I had also deceived myself that I was giving up drinking for someone else in an effort to get praise. I hadn't yet understood that giving up drinking was for *myself*, for *my* own good!

From then on, I observed that this mental state was my deadliest enemy and it is probably yours. Being able to recognize it is *all-important*. The lack of recognition of this in your personality will keep you from sobriety. Right now take a minute and try to think about times you drank and what went before it. Analyze your feelings, especially when you have had a I-don't-give-a-damn feeling or the I'll-show-them feeling or, perhaps, it was the who-the-hell-cares feeling.

This is one kind of self-deception. But there is another kind that is just as deadly. It is the self-deception of the drink that "no one will notice." Actually very few people care if you make a fool of yourself, because you seem to have chosen that option. They will simply leave you in disgust.

Many years ago, after I had first been in AA for only a few months, my parents had a party and a great deal of whiskey was around. One of the guests asked me to refreshen a drink for him. I agreed but when I was confronted with all that whiskey, I'd decided I'd have a quick one (to see what it tasted like!). "What difference would it make?" *No one would know.*

70

As I was furtively tossing off the shot, I realized that I wasn't fooling *them* but I was fooling myself. My mind had made up the delusion, the self-deception, to keep me from knowing the truth until it was too late.

The alcoholic's mind is a computer of rationalizations, guaranteed to fool even the most astute. This computerized mind holds several rationalizations for every kind of occasion. The woman who is serious about overcoming this personality flaw *must* bend, fold, and mutilate them, every last rationalization.

The most difficult part of all this, of course, is to be able to recognize the rationalizations before it is too late. As alcoholics we have used them for many years, as many years as we have been drinking. These rationalizations are an integral part of the personality we must reshape. But what are these? Will you recognize them now?

1. "After I get dried out, I'll be able to handle drinking." (So will the coroner.)
2. "No one will notice me taking this one." (That's true.)
3. "I'll just have one." (You bet!)
4. "I'm so up tight, one drink can't hurt." (That's true, too.)
5. "I don't want to be the only one not drinking." (!)
6. "What will people say if I don't drink?" (They'll shake your hand. You've probably spoiled many of their evenings.)
7. "I don't give a damn about anything. I don't care if I stay drunk forever." (It's expensive and unpleasant at the end.)
8. "I feel so low when I'm not drinking. That's the only time I feel alive." (Vitamins and three meals a day will change that.)
9. "Nobody cares for me." (Probably not as you are, but as soon as you care for them, they will reciprocate.)
10. "I'll just have one for the road." (That's all, sister.)
11. "I think better when I have a drink." (No comment.)

In the first months of sobriety, you will find these phrases still coming to mind frequently. Getting rid of them is, perhaps, the most difficult part of getting, and staying, sober.

These phrases, and the feelings that accompany them, have been with us too long to be exorcised in a short time. It will take constant vigilance on your part. Without recognizing and changing these attitudes in the very beginning, you will be right back on your treadmill to oblivion.

How many times I found myself drinking, wondering how it happened. Thinking back, I could always pinpoint the moment when I suddenly felt worthless or when life seemed empty or I felt that no one cared a damn. Talking to other alcoholic women, I have found that they, too, felt the same way. If your past efforts at stopping drinking ended in an abysmal failure, more than likely it was because you permitted a sense of inadequacy and self-pity to reign. Most alcoholic women have extremely low ego profiles.

Your program must include a mental remake. Your desire to be a new person is dependent upon your ability to recognize and shed these unlovable, weak characteristics.

As the days of sobriety begin to add up and your self-respect begins to return, be ever cautious of that day when someone's casual remark can still set off a chain of thoughts like "Who the hell does he think he is?" or "Who the hell cares if I'm sober?" These are big danger signals.

There will be no Greek chorus singing your praises all the time. Perhaps now you can see why it is extremely important to be among the friends who are happy for you, and to be around people who praise you for exerting will power, effort, and determination in not taking that first drink.

Resentments are not easily discarded. They are buried deep within us. Don't be naïve enough to believe that, once you have stopped drinking, upsetting days will be ended. There will always be situations which permit you to deceive yourself. I've known drinkers who have stopped drinking but haven't changed one iota of personality. Most are never happy nor do they have constant sobriety.

There are times, in fact, when resentments become stronger

after sobriety, since most resentments stem from deep-seated fears that once were subdued by alcohol. These fears include:

Fear of not being loved
Fear of failure
Fear of indebtedness
Fear of being unpopular
Fear of not being attractive to others
Fear of old age
Fear of death
Fear of incurable illness
Fear of balding and wrinkles
Fear of losing teeth
Fear of being without money

Fears such as these frequently turn into resentments. We resent those who seem to have everything, we resent the beautiful, the rich, the well-loved, believing that we are incapable of having any of their rewards.

Many people suffer from these fears: those who overeat, bite nails, have ulcers and hemorrhoids, can't sleep, have asthma, drive too fast, are on drugs, spend millions on diets and beauty aids, those who travel without cessation and those who are buried in work. The alcoholic's fears, although the same, are turned into resentments.

Alcoholics' fears are flamed by an inordinate tendency to worry. As the disease progresses, so do the fears, since every time the effect of the alcohol wears off, depression and fear set in.

Eventually you will learn how to be with people who drink and it will not bother you. It won't be at first, but it will happen after you have made some personality adjustments. In the beginning, however, keep away from places where you are not yet on safe ground. It will make your sobriety a difficult period and in addition will make you resentful at first.

If the occasion arises that you are around people who are drinking, I warn you now, never say, "I'm sorry I don't drink,

I'm an alcoholic." This seems to set people to laughing and coaxing you to have a drink: "Just one won't hurt."

Recently I was in an airport bar with a friend who is a drinking alcoholic. Some young men offered to buy us a drink. My friend ordered a vodka martini and I ordered ginger ale. At once the young men said, "Ah, come *on, have* a drink!" So I used the only line I have found, over the years, that works: "Oh, I'd love to but my ulcer is killing me." Quickly one of them said, "Oh, that's too bad." He was genuinely caring and the episode was ended.

It has taken me a number of incidents to find out that that line works. For some reason, a nondrinker is a peculiar bird and a nondrinking alcoholic is even more strange. The nondrinking alcoholic is coaxed, derided, and becomes an object to be convinced that her alcoholism just isn't so. The coaxers are usually men, although other women have been known to engage in this sport.

There are few drinking Americans who view the nondrinking alcoholic seriously. Moreover the social drinker has not the slightest idea of what the nondrinking alcoholic went through to achieve nondrinking status. Not to drink in the United States is akin to being a nonperson unless you claim an ulcerous condition, probably because so many persons in high places suffer from ulcers brought about by aggression and tension. Ulcers have become fashionably acceptable.

In any event, save yourself some heartbreak and embarrassment and stay away from drinking people. After a space of time you will notice that most of these people have little to say, and you will wonder how you ever spent so many wasted hours in their company, thinking them the epitome of sophistication and intellectuality.

Another experience of mine is exactly to this point. I was invited to a Sunday dinner party where everyone had a doctor's degree in one field or another. I was the only one not drinking, although I kept up with tomato juice with a dash of Worcestershire sauce. A lovely many-course dinner was prepared but, by the time we ate, several hours late, the dinner was dry and the guests were unable to taste what they were eating.

Dinner was followed with brandy. By this time I was so bored I could barely wait to leave. I had been there five hours and I wondered how I could possibly have engaged in events of this kind. Several years before I would have come away drunk and convinced that I had had a great time involved in brilliant conversation. Instead, I saw intelligent people become childish, maudlin, and boring.

In your new life, you will:

1. Eat differently.
2. Think differently.
3. Act differently.

You will have to fill the vacuum left from not drinking. At first you will find it hard to believe how much time you have or how much your mind was once totally preoccupied with drinking and the thought of it.

But it will be a whole new life, one of promise and peace.

Chapter 5

I was in a hospital for ten days. In that time I began to dry out and to learn some nasty truths, things I really knew but didn't want to know. After ten days I again felt human and wanted to get out. Sylvia told me my car was ready and I was all set to go back to my schedule of the job and everything else. The dissertation. All the parts of my life. I was sure that now I had to give up drinking. And I wanted to. I was ashamed and felt humiliation for what I had done, for being in the hospital, for having lost control of myself and my life.

I just wanted to be out and gone. I'd never see these people again and would never have to feel this humiliation.

Dr. Z. came into the room, looking serious and about to give a lecture, which he did. He looked at me with disgust, as most medical people do with alcoholics, for they view it as a waste of time.

"I suppose Dr. E. has told you what we've found?" he asked perfunctorily.

I put my arms behind my head in a semigesture of defiance. "No. Was he supposed to?"

"Well, I thought he might have," he countered. Pulling a chair away from the wall and closer to the bed, he sat down and ruffled through the papers on his clipboard. He wasn't a young man but he also wasn't old. He seemed all medicine and nothing else. I wondered how someone could be so consumed with one thing. I was always suspicious that there were problem areas in a dedicated life of such totality.

"You're just not in very good shape physically, but I don't suppose that's very new to you, is it?"

He looked directly at me but with no emotion showing.

"No, it's not new." I took my arms away from behind my head and interlocked my fingers on the cover top. "I want to quit but somehow I can't seem to."

His eyes warmed up and he looked concerned. "There isn't much hope if you don't. Your liver is shot, your gall bladder, you have an ulcer, and there are other problems although more minor."

The news of my liver shocked me. Never before had there been evidence of trouble. "Do I have cirrhosis?"

"Yes. But why does that shock you?"

I was silent, trying to absorb all of it. It was as if the person who drank all those years was someone else and now this doctor was telling me the news about that other person. But it seemed that it was me. Me! I began to cry silently.

"I don't see why this comes as such a shock!" he said with some exasperation. "No one can drink the quantities you did and not pay for it. Actually, you've been very lucky. I don't know how you've managed this long with just this amount of damage."

I began remembering the warnings I'd had all along, warnings I had always ignored and forgotten. And there had been many. Alcoholic poisoning, brain damage, internal bleeding . . .

"This can all be alleviated by a cessation of drinking. No more alcohol ever. This should serve as a good lesson to you. The drinking days are over."

He reached over and patted my hand and left.

I had to get out. I couldn't stay in this prison. I felt threatened and deserted. And alone. Always alone, no one to care really. In all the time I was in the hospital Sylvia alone came to see me every day. No, I was never alone as long as Sylvia continued to show her steadfast devotion. And what had I ever done to show her that I appreciated her caring?

Again the self-pity, remorse, guilt, humiliation, depression. I

77

had to run, get away, begin over again somewhere where no one knew me. I'd leave the hospital and then sell everything, my farm, and everything except my car. And I'd go to some small town in the West and begin again. But alone? Knowing no one?

Oh, I hated hospitals. The very atmosphere forced one to think about beginnings and endings, about practical solutions for medical problems. Wonder how many people decide to buy insurance when in here? Or make funeral arrangements?

Cirrhosis, eh? I was really stunned, for I'd always had the peculiar and unreasonable feeling that nothing would ever happen to me. I had always felt special, anointed, set aside for unusual treatment and favors. Now I felt as if God had abandoned me.

If I really thought about it I could see that all of the gyrations in my thinking were rationalizations to lead me from the truth and reality. I wanted to escape the responsibility of my actions.

I thrashed around in bed, feeling uncomfortable with truth as a bed partner. I sat up and I practically leaped out of bed. I was really feeling wonderful. No headache, no shakes, no more nausea, no more thickness in my body. I was almost slim again. I felt a great joy surge through me. How wonderful to be alive!

Grabbing my terry-cloth robe, I left the room and started walking the halls. It was almost time for Sylvia, who came every day after work and stayed until visitors had to leave. How could she? She worked eight hours in a hospital and then came here and stayed with me in another hospital for four more hours! And I thought I was the anointed one!

There she was, getting off the elevator, looking happy and as if she really enjoyed coming here. I watched her look at the patients and there was real concern on her face for them. Then I looked at them collectively and felt nothing. Oh, I didn't want anyone to suffer but I couldn't feel concern. Was I really so uncaring? I knew that that wasn't really true but it also wasn't untrue.

"Syl, here I am," I called to her.

78

She was smiling as she walked toward me. "Don't you look good."

"I feel alive and happy and ready for anything."

"You look it. Have you seen the doctor? When can you go home?"

"Probably tomorrow. Where is my car?"

"I had them take it to the farm. Is that O.K.?"

"Sure. How will I get there?" .

"I'll drive you. Let's find out when."

We sat in the lounge and talked for a long while before I saw my own doctor go to my room.

"There's Dr. E. I'll ask him."

"O.K. I'll stay here and talk to some of the patients."

How in the world *could* she? Shrugging my shoulders, I went to my room and just caught him.

"There you are. Did Dr. Z. talk to you?" George asked, looking quizzical.

"Yes. Can I go home tomorrow?"

"I'd really like you to stay awhile and give yourself some real recuperation time. Each day is important."

"I know, but there is so much for me to do. I have so many things coming due." And then the hearing popped into my head and I broke into perspiration. Oh, no, not that all over again.

"Will you begin to live like a sane and sober person, Jean? You know, you're at the end. Your body can't stand it anymore. And you're not that young either."

I almost laughed out loud. I had never thought of myself as being "older"! It struck me as being unreal. "Not young anymore?" Ridiculous! Maybe that's how I thought myself different. Ageless.

"Look, George, I'm going home and be the model patient. No more drinking. No more running away. No more anything that spells trouble. I know I've got to get with it. I intend to do that."

He scrutinized me carefully and seemed to see that I wasn't as cunning or conning as I most often was.

"All right, you can leave tomorrow. I'll sign you out. And I want to see you in my office regularly. We'll keep you on vitamins and a medication for your sluggish thyroid."

Brother, that was new. When did I get a sluggish thyroid? But I wasn't about to ask.

"Thanks, George."

He smiled and then left.

Before joining Sylvia, I looked out the large hospital window for a long minute. Obviously I wasn't looking at life right. I wasn't managing it. Better go to Syl.

As I came upon her, she was encouraging someone to do something in knitting.

"Here I am. Discharged. Well, tomorrow I'll be discharged."

She looked at me. "You really look good, Jean. I don't know when you last looked this way."

"I feel great." And I did. But the hearing began to nag at me.

"What's wrong?"

We're like most people who have known each other for years and read the other's mind.

"I just thought about the hearing."

"Well, don't think of that now. When the time comes, you appear and explain. They'll either take your license or not."

Well, that's a damn practical viewpoint. Now I'll tell my emotional system what to feel!

"Isn't that right?" she persisted.

"Sure it's right, if I could only get the rest of me to adopt that attitude."

The bell had rung for the visitors to leave.

"Guess that's my exit. I'll arrange for tomorrow and take you home. It's usually about ten o'clock that you can leave."

I watched her walk down the corridor to the elevator. Again she acknowledged people and smiled at them, sometimes making a comment to them. It was evidently instinctual with her, this caring for others.

I walked into the lounge and sat on a chair next to an older woman and waited. She was looking all around the lounge and sort of let her eyes and ears linger on the conversations of others. I wanted to get her attention to ask her how she felt but I didn't know how to do it. I stared at her but she never looked my way. Disgusted with my unsuccessful attempt at personal public relations, I went back to my room. I was restless. I began to think about drinking. There was a feeling inside me that made me want to drink but I wasn't craving it. Just thinking about it. Now I would never be sick again. Could I really have felt as bad as I thought I had? I began to see the last weeks of my life and I wanted to cringe, to hide. How disgusting! To think I let myself become animalistic. Crawling, sleeping on the floor, dirty clothes from up-chucking . . .

I put it all out of my mind. I felt shame for what I'd let myself become. I wanted to run, but there was no place to run to. No place for a drink. Trapped. Perspiration began to pour from me.

Walking back to my room as rapidly as I could, I spied a wall phone and decided to call my parents to tell them I'd be home tomorrow. I hadn't seen them since I'd been in the hospital these ten days.

I dialed and the phone rang many times. No one home. I was disappointed.

This would certainly be a long night. What to do with the time? Maybe I'd try to think about putting the pieces together, but my thoughts always came up against the hearing. I still didn't know when it would be but that didn't change much.

My room was very quiet. I sat in a chair next to the window that looked out on a beautiful lawn. There was a great sense of peace out there that seemed to want to spread itself over me but which I turned away from. It was all so unreal. The emotions inside me were all struggling for expression. I felt like I wanted to sing or to shout or to run or to dance. There was a wildness in me that had always seemed part of my being. As long as I could remember, it was there, urging me to do what others did not.

Abruptly I arose and let out a long sigh. It would be nice to relax here with a drink. Oh no, no more of that, Jean. Time's up. This time you've really hit the jackpot. If you wanted to cash in your chips, you darn near made it, didn't you?

But how would I manage the whole of it? Maybe I'd go back to AA but I'd be sober this time. That's the only way I can possibly manage to keep my life in tow.

Right now I crawled between the clean sheets and tried to sleep. It was a long time coming, but finally I drifted into a restless half-consciousness that saw me through to daylight. Night always was a time of trauma for me, I was riddled by guilt feelings and I feared sleeping, as if I had gone into a nether world of dark figures and judgmental accusers.

I welcomed this last morning of hospital routine. After breakfast I packed my few clothes. It came as a surprise to me what I actually had, for I didn't remember being brought here or what I had been wearing. Oh, how good it will be to always know my actions and never have to worry about where I've been or what I've said or what I've done! It seemed so strange to awaken and be able to leap out of bed without being sick, without my head feeling as if it would break in two. Ah, the advantages of the good life, never to be discounted.

Having said good-bye to the few nurses who were civil, I went to the lounge and awaited Sylvia. I thought I'd try my sociological experiment in personal relations again.

I took a seat next to a younger woman this time. She was smoking and seemed very upset.

"Hi," I began lamely.

She looked at me and said a weak "Hi."

"It's a nice day, isn't it?" I asked.

"Guess so." With that, she got up and went out of the room to meet a patient from another floor.

Disgusted, I decided that my attempts at being like Sylvia in relation to people were at an end.

"I see you're ready. Let's go," Sylvia said, having come in at just that minute. "I'll bet you're glad to get out of here, aren't you?"

"You know it. Wait, I'll get my bag."

I got my bag and we left the hospital for her car, parked right out in front.

It was so good to be out. I took deep breaths of air. How good it all was.

Our drive home was very short, only twenty minutes. Syl wasn't able to stay but said she'd call that night. When we drove into the lane, there stood my car, a beautiful sight, all back into perfect shape, as if nothing had ever happened.

When Syl left I got into my car and started it. It was just like new. Well, it *was* new, not more than a few months old. I drove out the lane and to my parents' home eight blocks away. My dad's car was gone but maybe my mother was home. Using my key, I went in, but the house was silent and empty. I looked for a note telling me where they were, but there was none, since they didn't know I was out of the hospital.

I went to the liquor cabinet and looked in. There was every kind of liquor there. I looked at it long and hard. Then I closed the door and left the room and the house, my heart beating quite fast. That was a close one, Jean.

I drove back to my farm and unpacked my hospital suitcase. The house was a mess, so I began to clean. Everywhere there was evidence of my last days of drinking. I gathered dirty clothes, changed the bed sheets, and went to a laundromat and did the laundry. Then I did the dishes and soon had the house in such a sparkling condition I knew no one would recognize it.

I wanted to call someone to come visit, but everyone I thought of would be drinking and would expect a drink. So I gave up that idea.

Before the afternoon was over I had all the work finished. I had even collected the empty bottles and thrown them into the trash can, not caring how many there were. I had made a new resolution and, in doing so, I had to break with the past cleanly.

Bravo, Jean.

Time began to hang heavy. I didn't know what to do with myself, and I felt restless. I wanted to get on with life. I wanted it to move without my suffering. And I didn't want to do any of the obvious things I had to do: get back to my job, finish a paper for Lehigh, finish writing my dissertation, and decide what I would do with my future, the whole rest of my life.

I called my parents again before watching the evening news.

No one home. So I fixed myself a tuna-fish salad and got myself before the TV set. The food tasted very good, and I savored each bite. It had been years since I enjoyed food like this. My taste buds were coming alive again and everything I ate was a new experience.

A half hour later, I was restless. Time hung in clusters of boredom. What to do?

I got into my car and went to see Judy and John. They were preparing dinner and having a drink . . . drinks.

"You look great. Where have you been?" Judy asked the minute she saw me.

"Hi. Oh, I was out of town for ten days."

John came into the room. "Wherever you've been, you look great."

"I feel good."

"What can I get for you to drink?" he asked, already walking to the bar.

"Nothing, thanks. I must run along and see my parents. I was just passing and wanted to say hello."

I prepared to leave.

"Can't you stay just a few moments more? You just got here," Judy insisted.

But I had to get away. I couldn't stand the temptation or watching the way it used to be. How would I ever live without drinking? It seemed not possible.

I left in a big hurry, barely being civil in my good-byes. I wanted to stay, to drink and enjoy the conviviality of their friendship, but I couldn't do it not drinking.

I drove home slowly but first went to my parents' house. Again no one home, gone the entire day.

So I drove around town, feeling like a stranger in a familiar place. What was my life going to be like? What indeed. Boredom, restlessness, friendless? And who the hell said I had to stop drinking? What did they know? Their damn tests could be wrong. Nothing's wrong with me. I look good, feel good. And who cares anyway?

I drove to the liquor store and bought a quart of whiskey. Driving home, I thought about what I'd done and wasn't the least bit disappointed in myself. I was just damned agitated with everyone.

The bottle seemed bigger than I had remembered. Brother, what will I do with all this liquor? Maybe I should have gotten a pint. Ah well, you can always keep it, it doesn't spoil!

I poured a small amount in a glass, added ice and club soda. Then I waited minutes before drinking it. Well, here goes!

I drank very slowly. Oh, it tasted delicious. How could anything that tasted so good do what *they* said?

I didn't want to drink fast. I had made it very light and easy. Almost no liquor in it.

I made another and it tasted almost as good as the first.

I spent the night watching TV and had a very pleasant evening, drinking leisurely and not letting it get out of control. By the eleven o'clock news I was very pleased with myself and went to bed.

The night sounds were very pleasing. I listened closely to the sound of the night's silence and found it almost comforting. Rather quickly I fell asleep but toward early morning I awoke and felt very uneasy. I began to think about the problems of my life and the internal churning began. I tossed and rolled and tossed some more, but sleep and peace alluded me. I got up and walked through the quiet house, looking for the clock. At last I was able to see it and found it to be 3:30 A.M. of the day I had to call Nick and get back to work and call Walter about the people I hit in the accident. I thought of my dissertation and the work yet to be done for my classes at Lehigh and what I would be able to do when I was finished, which, at the moment, seemed like nothing at all, that, after all these years, my education added up to zilch.

I went to the kitchen in the darkness and poured a drink, a stiff drink neat, nothing on the side. This time I wasn't fooling around. I wanted to get drunk, I wanted out.

As I leaned against the sink counter drinking it, a faint light appeared in the fields outside the kitchen windows. It came from an industrial plant across the field and the eerie light from the open flame was hypnotizing. I watched it and wondered if I could simply have everything go away by being absorbed by this strange light. Again I was conscious of the stillness and my being surrounded by the four walls of the house, as if they were wrapped around me in the form of a trap.

I shook myself away from those thoughts and poured another drink. Cirrhosis, eh? So what? It just wasn't me those medical giants were talking about. Someone else. How could it be me? I was the same now as before. Sure, there were times when I couldn't manage the liquor, but that happens to everyone, doesn't it? Just get too much and my system can't metabolize it. Pure and simple, that's all.

But a cold chill ran down my spine, thinking about cirrhosis. Had I blown the whole thing? Rot! I kept on drinking and wanted oblivion. The liquor was beginning to hit me and I felt carefree and on top of the entire world. I felt capable of handling everything that came along. Even though it was still night, I got out the papers for my dissertation and looked at them very carefully. No reason why I couldn't work now, none at all. But the notes made little sense to me. Instead, the bulk of them threatened me, intimidated me with their look of authority and demand for more quality work.

With a quick movement, my hand swept all the papers on the floor with all of the three-by-five cards scattering over the room.

I stumbled to the kitchen and got the bottle and then turned on a radio very loudly. I began to sing and shout, feeling free and exultant. If only I could express this intense feeling of power. There must be a way!

Looking at the dining room in the faint light of dawn, I decided I'd paint it. Rushing to the back porch, I found some yellow paint and a brush. As I removed the top and started to stir it, thinking what fun I'd have, my arm touched the can and it spilled over the floor. Oh, what the hell! I cursed and grabbed some dishtowels to wipe up the mess as best I could. Bending over, I fell forward and had trouble righting myself. But did.

The radio blared a song I especially liked and I sang at the top of my lungs, as if happiness were a dominant force in my life.

Then I fell over in a heap and gave in to the liquor. I felt very ill but knew I had to drink but didn't know why. The bottle was there beside me and I had to finish it, always had to finish it.

I began vomiting but couldn't help myself. I knew I was sick, sick, sick, but I didn't care. I wanted only to die, to be away from life yet not totally dead.

Oh, God, oh God, oh God, help me again.

I rolled away from my sickness but could not get up. Or crawl. Stupor took over and, hours later, I was awakened by the phone on the wall above my head. I tried to get up but took minutes to do so. By then the phone had stopped ringing. I began to see the mess of everything and I couldn't believe any of it. The executive woman, the success story, the achiever. Whoops, the overachiever, isn't that what I'm called? Mustn't forget an important thing like that.

The phone rang again. It was Walter.

"See you're home from the hospital."

"Yes," I mumbled.

"Are you there?" he asked.

"Sure, I'm here. What's the problem?"

"You're damn lucky. Those people you hit are insured by us and they don't want to appear anywhere with any case against you. I have a feeling they have something to hide. In any case, they have signed off and will not bring charges. How's that to start your day?"

"Great." Slowly it began to come to me what he was talking about. The accident. The big accident. The hit-and-run. Now it began to make some sense. See, you worried for nothing. Well, I'll drink to that.

"Did you hear what I said? Nothing to worry about."

"Walter, you're terrific. I'll see you later this week."

"O.K. Keep your nose clean." He hung up.

Keep my nose clean? That's about all that was. I looked at myself in utter disgust. The filth. Then the old retching began and I had to get a drink down. Back to the old routine. I began to cry in between the retching and trying to get to the bath-

87

room. But the entire effort was futile. Everywhere I looked there was filth and upset and paint and disarray and stench.

Oh, God, help me again. I'll never drink again. Never, never, never. I was so good when I got out of the hospital. When was that? What day is it? What must I do with the rest of my life after I find out what day and what time it is? Who must I see? Where must I go?

Somehow a number of truths began to come to me. If I was going to make it, I had to do it alone. I was really alone, no matter what anyone said. We are all alone. We are born alone, live alone, die alone. That is an inescapable truth. And I knew that the way I was going about not living was sure as hell the most painful way possible. I began to see that all I was doing was making myself too sick to carry out life's functions yet not sick enough to die.

All this in a quick flash as I managed to get to the bathroom. I had to get myself cleaned and together and begin to work at life. That much I knew. The "how" of it I didn't know.

Struggling out of my clothes, retching, perspiring, feeling excessively dizzy, green and yellow all at one time, I removed my clothes as best I could. Today had to be the day.

I got into a tub of hot water and suds and soaked for half an hour, fighting the nausea. I also washed my hair, yet I still felt dirty and disgusting. But I knew it was me, myself, with whom I was disgusted, who I couldn't stand.

Shakily and with much effort, I dried myself, falling several times but getting right back to it. I began to think of what I had to do but my head was cracking in two.

Why did I go to all this trouble to get sick again when I had to reverse the process and come back? Why?

Chapter 6

Several days later I was recovered enough to get back to the turnpike driving and to my job. I was happy that I had been so sick, because it made not drinking that much easier.

But I was obsessed with thoughts of drinking. There was a big void in my life that I had to fill. I also had to learn how to tackle my problem. It began to get to me that I had to quit drinking, not just taper off. How I would do it was still a mystery. My call to AA had resulted in an agreement to go to a meeting tonight. I was very nervous as I waited for Ruth, the woman to whom I'd spoken over the phone. She was going to pick me up and we were going to a small town nearby.

While waiting for her, I thought about having a shot but didn't. I began to realize that my mental addiction seemed to be much worse than my physical addiction. Right at the minute my body was perfectly satisfied with not drinking. But my mind was not. Only my thoughts were creating this turmoil and craving at this moment.

A horn sounded in the driveway and it was Ruth. I grabbed my handbag and ran out the door.

She was a young woman whose illness was written all over her face. Her hands were shaking and she smoked endlessly, in an unbroken chain of cigarettes.

"Hi. So nice of you to come for me," I said as I got into the front seat of her car.

"My name is Ruth. So glad you could come along." She looked at me quickly.

As we drove to Perkasie, she chattered nervously and told me about herself. She had been "dry" for seven months but her uneasiness and her speech made it hard for me to believe. My earlier years in AA let me know that Ruth's sobriety was not a happy period. Was mine going to be like that?

We parked the car and climbed the steps to the second floor of an old union building. The small room was already smoke-filled. We were the only women in a room of about fifteen men. In minutes the meeting got under way and it all came back to me as if I had never been away. The stories and the rehash of the drinking years.

As I looked around, I saw Jerry, the man who had picked me up last year. He half-smiled at me, as if to say he knew I'd be back, so I was back! But I wasn't drunk, and I was glad for that part.

In an hour the meeting was over and most of the men came to me and introduced themselves and said they were happy to see me there and that they knew the "program" would work if I wanted it to. Even Jerry said much the same, noting that I looked better and seemed better than when he had seen me.

Ruth's duties as secretary kept her busy until it was time for us to leave. On the way home, she again talked nervously, telling me how hard it was for her to stay sober. The meeting had created drinking thoughts for me and I wanted to be home with a bottle, away from all these people.

When we drove in the lane, I thanked Ruth and invited her in. She wanted to get home to her family and said she'd come some other time.

As I let myself into the house, I thought about the meeting and what was said. Somehow, it didn't give me what I needed to make it. Maybe it was because I was so familiar with the program, having lived it night and day for three years before. Could that be?

But I didn't think so. I just felt that my sobriety needed to have more ways for me to grow. Obviously I was not a mature human being nor was I a rounded woman. I didn't especially feel like a woman. I didn't feel like much of anything, my idea of myself being very unclear. I was Jean, whoever she was . . . a disturbed, immature, unsure-of-self woman. Middle-aged besides. Brother! There would be no picnic in putting this Humpty Dumpty back together again. Back together again? Was I ever together? Oh, for a drink!

The empty house brought back unpleasant memories of recent bouts. I almost hated it but decided that now was the time to make a real stand for what I had to do.

The police hearing was set for the end of the week. Sylvia was coming to be with me that day in between her packing to leave for Florida and a new job. She would stay at the house with me. I wanted to tell her that I was going to make the sobriety trail this time but decided against it, since I had disappointed her so many times before. We spoke on the phone almost every day but I said nothing and she didn't ask except for inquiring about my health.

I walked from room to room before going to bed. Would living with someone end this churning inside me? What did I really want? If only I knew what life was all about, mine in particular.

I remembered how I had loved reading Emerson so I found my book and, after putting on my night clothes, crawled into bed and began reading. I began to read "Nature" and became totally absorbed. I felt excited about what I was reading. My mind began to function on a new wavelength and, for the moment, the thought of the drink that was tantalizing me was put aside.

I read, "To speak truly, few adult persons can see nature. Most persons do not see the sun. At least they have a very superficial seeing. The sun illuminates only the eye of the man, but shines into the eye and the heart of the child."

I put the book aside and sat in bed, trying to think about my own observation of nature. I remembered it had been a nice day. Well, there was no rain! Great observation, Jean.

I picked up the book and read on: "In the woods, we return to reason and faith. There I feel that nothing can befall me in life—no disgrace, no calamity (leaving me my eyes), which nature cannot repair. Standing on the bare ground—my head bathed by the blithe air and uplifted into infinite space—all mean egotism vanishes."

Again I put the book aside. Powerful stuff. I had always thought so during my college years but now the message began to get to my brain and I thought about it with some real seriousness.

When was the last time I had noticed the natural environment in which I lived? Well, I saw it when I drove to Philadelphia or Wilkes-Barre. Did I? I couldn't remember much except that Wilkes-Barre was uphill and Philadelphia was downhill. Another great observation. But was I always so oblivious to what went on around me?

Thoughts and emotions churned. I wanted it to be daylight so that I could experiment. But it was nighttime and I had to get to sleep to get to work. Plenty of time for observation tomorrow on the turnpike. And the hearing coming up in two days.

I put out the light and tossed for hours. It occurred to me that I was a very upset and unhappy person. What was I really like?

Dawn soon appeared and then I fell asleep for a few hours. When I finally arose and dressed, I was extremely tired and without the enthusiasm I had felt only hours earlier. Maybe a drink would get me going.

Toying with the idea, I went to the kitchen and had a quick drink. It tasted horrible and almost made me sick. I looked for some food to get the taste out of my mouth and found only stale bread, which I ate in the hope that it would remove the bitterness. It didn't, but it helped. It also helped the new churning in my stomach from the drink.

Oh, Jean, you are a disgusting lot.

I left the house on that sour note and drove the turnpike, thinking only about drinking and that I might have one or two when I got home from work in just a few hours.

My obsession with the thought of drinking plagued me the entire trip to the office. Entirely gone from my consciousness was the thought of observing nature and the environment in which I lived.

The morning dragged along. There were new rumors of the contract not being renewed with HEW. But that was so often heard that I didn't worry about it. From our work schedule, however, I knew that something was in the air. No longer was I pressed to prepare textbooks in two months. In fact, there was little actual new work for me. My biggest assignment was to keep busy by devising jobs for myself. And that bored me to death. It was like rearranging the furniture on a sinking ship. Why not get off and start anew? That's what I really wanted to do but all my recent debts kept me from it. I was especially disgusted with myself that I would stay on just to collect a big paycheck for doing something any file clerk could do. I loathed the enslavement of money, yet I was just like all those others who disgusted me by staying in a nonproductive job just for the money.

Nick came over to my desk. I worked hard at looking busy.

"Can you go along to lunch? Dick is here with the new proposal." He began to turn away, knowing, of course, that I would go . . . had to go.

"I'll be ready anytime."

I began to look forward to lunch, for my head was splitting and my hands were beginning to show a tremor. My body was coming away from alcohol very slowly.

Nick called, "We're ready now."

I rose and joined the men. I knew that something was expected of me, otherwise I wouldn't have been asked to go along. I was the only woman in the office not in a clerical or secretarial position, yet I was always excluded from all meetings that were with everyone in the office in key positions, despite this being an educational firm and I was the only one at the doctoral level. I supposed many times that that was why my outrageous behavior was tolerated, because my educational background looked good in proposals.

Again I felt disgust for myself for not speaking out more often about this inequality but I didn't because of my frequent absences and general undependability. Why call attention to it? Why give Nick a chance to point it out?

We drove to a nearby cocktail lounge and Dick monopolized the conversation with his high-sounding jargon of proposals. It appeared as though I was to work with him and do the proposal writing. I was dreading the assignment because I didn't like Dick. I always thought him full of hot air.

As we sat down to order, Nick was saying, "Maybe you can go to Washington and work with Dick, Jean."

"Sure. Glad to." I fell into the corporate geniality easily, but I was very upset. Washington indeed. To work with Dick no less!

"What shall we have before lunch?" Nick asked.

Dick ordered his usual margarita, Nick had a scotch, since he rarely drank and didn't even like it. I hesitated for just a split second and then ordered a manhattan. What the hell! Why stand out in the crowd?

The drinks were served quickly. Funny that food never had the same fast route. I drank mine very slowly, sipping it in fact. While the buzz of the men's voices went all around me, I played at being a normal drinker, holding the glass casually, trying to be uninterested in it, looking uninterestedly at the crowd, posing as just a woman who drank for something to do but really didn't like what she was drinking.

See, not bad at all. I began to believe that I could handle the scene from now on. No more binges, just a cocktail here and there, drink slowly and without craving.

I heard my name and had to force my attention back to the conversation. What was I doing here with these men? Everything was a drudge, yet I had to play the game. That's what it seemed like to me.

"Yes?"

"It's all settled then. The target date will be a month from today."

My playing someone else with the drink had removed me so entirely from the present conversation that I had no real idea of what they were talking about.

"O.K., we can do it." Well said, Jean. Display confidence and certainty. "Are we having another before ordering?" I asked as nonchalantly as I could.

"If you'd care to," Nick said. He ordered for me and, at the last minute, Dick decided to have another margarita. I tried not to realize that the men wouldn't have had another had I not asked for one. Oh well, so what.

Nick started ordering and I drank my drink quickly. My, but it tasted good that way, down fast and whap! I wanted another drink but knew I had to eat. Damn. I ordered. Then a great idea presented itself.

"Excuse me please," I murmured, as I stood up and acted as though I were trying to find the direction of the ladies' room with my eyes. I walked away from the table and indirectly made my way to a corner of the cocktail bar and ordered a straight Seagram's. Quickly I drank it and walked casually back to the table via a circuitous route, rubbing my hands together, as if I had just washed them in the lavatory and that was the reason for my leaving the group. I chuckled silently at my cleverness.

Our food had been served and I managed to get some of it eaten, although my mind was aflame with thoughts of leaving the office and getting to a bottle as quickly as possible.

Our trip to the office was uneventful and Dick seemed not especially interested in discussing future plans with me nor was I with him. I knew he'd call the same day he wanted to see me. Considerate.

I marveled at the way I was able to be in the group of five men, seem to look interested, yet not be there at all. My mind roved from thoughts of the bottle I'd buy to getting away from it all for several weeks.

We left the car and entered the office.

"O.K., Dick. Let us know when you're coming back or when you want to see Jean," Nick was saying.

Quickly the good-byes to Dick were said and we all went to our various desks. I noted that Dick was not at all enthusiastic about working with me. So that made two of us!

I waited a half hour before gathering my things and leaving. Fire me, just fire me! My car was parked just a few feet from a liquor store. I wondered if I could go into it and not be seen from the office. Ah, who cares?

I went in and bought a pint. No sense in getting more with my controlled drinking schedule. And with my new attitude about drinking, I had no need for more.

The drive home began to take on a pleasant aspect. I opened the bottle and drove with it propped against me on the front seat. Every ten miles I took a long drink. Controlled drinking. The kind of sensible drinking that took into account the nature of the problem. Unfortunately there were more miles than I had whiskey to last for.

In Quakertown I went to the liquor store and got another pint. Maybe I'd save it for guests in the next few weeks.

At the house I decided to have a slow drink and made a lovely big highball . . . ice and soda and all the trappings, just right for TV watching.

I settled in front of the TV set and began a night's drinking and watching but an hour later I began to feel green and nauseated. I couldn't manage to keep my drink in my stomach and I began the retching routine. Oh, no. Not again, I thought, while I ran to the bathroom and made it just in time. The waves rolled over me and I thought they would never end. Ten minutes later I was drained of every liquid in my body, or so it seemed. My clothes were soaked, my hair was dripping wet, and I was totally spent, unable to rise from my kneeling position in front of the john.

In addition to feeling miserable, I was surprised at this strange reaction. What had happened? I began to think that the whiskey was bad. Maybe something got into it that I couldn't tolerate.

Exhausted, I crawled into bed and fell asleep almost immediately. And then it was the day before the police hearing. Sylvia called and said she would go along with me, which was a great relief.

I dressed slowly and carefully the next day. It was a great relief not to be sick or to have a hangover, although I wanted a drink. Mentally, I wanted a drink. Funny how that works, I thought. Sometimes my body was screaming for a drink, and, other times, I wanted a drink because my mind told me that it would give me a shot of confidence. But now I had had several days of rest.

Anyway, this morning I was very nervous but resigned to whatever the pronouncement might be. Or was I?

The door opened and Syl came in, smiling and the picture of health. She was very brunette and exuded confidence, the kind that is dependable in a crisis.

"You're looking good, Jean. Nervous?" she asked, looking at me with that special kind of examination reserved for nurses and close friends.

I smiled. "I really feel very good and I'm going to make it this time."

She just smiled and added no comment.

"I know you've heard that before, but I really am. Anyway, something has happened, I can't drink anymore." Then I told her what had happened to me the night before last.

"Everything is worn out in you. You're finished, I guess. Can't say that I'm unhappy about it."

"Where have you been these last few weeks?" I wondered aloud.

"Uh, I stayed away purposely. I thought that maybe I was always too handy for your own good."

"Perhaps."

"Let's go. It will take a half hour to get to the courthouse."

The drive was all too short. We managed to park in front of the courthouse and I asked Sylvia to wait. Slowly I walked in, as if walking into the hangman's noose.

Without too much trouble I found the room and there were several men gathered around a long table, which reminded me of my doctoral examinations many years before. The scene was much like this. Would it always be a table of men judging me? Where were the women in all of this?

Not one acknowledged my presence more than to lift eyes to mine. I took a chair and a deep breath. I smiled but not too much. They couldn't be conned, that was obvious.

"Good morning," I said briskly.

"Are you Mrs. Jean Kirkpatrick?"

"Yes."

"Did this accident occur on July the sixth at Hillmond and Market streets?"

"Yes."

"And did you leave the accident scene as so charged?"

"No, not as charged."

"Tell us what happened."

"After the accident occurred, I ran to the car and asked the occupants if they were hurt. They said no. With that, I got into my car and drove away."

They were observing me closely, trying to ascertain the truth, wondering if I spoke it. I worked hard at my expression and fought to control my hands so that the shaking did not show. To all appearances I was calm and poised.

"There somehow seems to be something missing in this entire account, but what it is we don't know. The Parsons refuse to press charges and so we must go by the account you have just given. You will know in a few days what the pronouncement is. Good day."

I was flabbergasted. It was over. Just like that. The inside of my clothes was soaking wet from the perspiration that was running down my body.

I arose and managed to keep myself together while nodding a crisp good-bye.

Outside the building, I took a deep breath. The air felt wonderful but I could smell the coming autumn. I was so glad it was over, so very, very glad. Why, there was nothing to it! What I did wasn't all that bad, for heaven's sake. Why was I so damn upset? Poof!

Sylvia's face reflected the concern she felt as I approached her car. Jauntily, I snapped my fingers and tossed my head. "Nothing to it. Just nothing to it."

She smiled. "I'm glad that's over before I leave for Florida."

Terror struck. "Are you still going? I thought you'd changed your plans."

"No, I'm going next week. The new job begins right away."

"Uh, I wasn't aware of it being so soon."

It felt as if a hole were put into the core of my life. It became more and more evident how much I depended upon Sylvia and her constant support. I wanted to drink, I wanted to be drunk. I wanted to be away from decisions, responsibilities, realities.

"Let's go," I said, my sense of freedom short-lived.

"Don't be upset. I'm not that far away. Anyway, it really is for the best—"

Rudely I cut into her words: "Best for whom? You? Me? How can it be best for me?" I asked sullenly.

"Wait and see. It's not good to have someone handy every time you want someone."

"Oh, nuts. You've been reading that alcoholic crap. I'm going to AA and I'm not drinking. What more do you want?"

"Let's not get into an argument. If we talk about it a month from now, I'm sure that you will see the difference," she said patiently.

I sulked for the rest of the drive home.

When we got to the farm, Sylvia suggested coming in but I didn't want her to stay. I had something else on my mind. The craving was beginning to drive me crazy and I was curt.

"You want to stay?"

"Not when you're like this. Anyway, I have packing to do."

"That again! You seem really eager," I said sarcastically.

"I am. I need new faces, and I need a new life."

"You mean you're tired of taking care of a drunk. How many years has it been? I met you in the hospital eleven years ago. Eleven years of baby-sitting. I'd guess that's enough for anyone. It's just not every friend one makes in a mental hospital, is it? And it isn't every mental patient that takes a decade of your time, is it?"

"Shut up, Jean. I'm going. I'll call you tomorrow."

"Go, damn it, go. I hope to hell I never see you again."

The instant rage welled up in me and I screamed at the top of my lungs. Damn, damn, damn, why do I always end up alone? Forever alone?

I watched her car leave the driveway and enter Heller Road. The pinch in my heart pinched more. I sighed.

I grabbed my car keys and went directly to the liquor store. Only a pint.

Before I got home, I tore open the wrappings on the bottle and took a big drink. It tasted like ambrosia.

At home, I went into the house and stood leaning against the kitchen sink. The bottle was in my hand and I began lifting it to my mouth but I drew it away. I began to think about everything that had happened. The pieces of my life that were lying in small piles of debris, waiting for me to dispose of the garbage, not to make more waste. It was all there for me to see, the mess I had created and continued to create.

Why did I want to drink? What was making me want to drink now? Suddenly it became apparent that I wanted to drink because I felt alone, I felt rejected, tossed aside by Sylvia. I felt unworthy, unloved, uncared for, yet, if I were honest, I was most definitely cared for. I pushed people to the greatest extremes and then challenged them not to leave me.

Strange. Very strange.

I put the bottle down and looked at it. Damn stuff. It had always represented the liquid of life and now it was that which destroyed me. But then I wanted to be destroyed. But why?

Why bother to think about it now? In a quick movement, I poured the liquor down the sink. Longingly I watched it. Another $4.00 shot. I consoled myself with the thought that the whole liquor store was full of more.

And then the rest of the day stretched out before me, awaiting my ambition to fill it. But I didn't want to do anything. I had stayed home from work to go to the hearing. Maybe I'd work on my dissertation.

I spent almost an hour making elaborate preparations to work on my dissertation. Carefully I placed the notes on the top of my desk. The filing cabinets of three-by-fives were placed at my fingertips. The carbon paper and typewriter were properly placed.

Then I was ready to begin but not one thought would enter my mind. The white paper in the roller of the typewriter threatened me, intimidated me. Which one? Or both?

I let my thoughts play with the absurd abstraction. And I

became aware of every sound of nature outside the window. The end of a season. The death, glorious death, of summer, cloaked in oranges and golds and browns.

Time slipped by me. When I turned back to my typewriter and my notes and all the paraphernalia of my dissertation I asked myself why I bothered with it when I didn't believe I could do it. Why go on? I forced myself to think about all the fellowships and honors that I'd won at the University of Pennsylvania. How had I conned all of them? It was just all a fluke. But what if I really could do it? I remembered that every time I had reports to give, it always went well. My papers always got an A. My class discussions were always rated tops. Who knows, maybe I could really do it.

I looked at the notes. Very obviously, there was something I wanted to say, that needed saying. I began to type and the words seemed to flow from me. Everything went well until I again began to doubt my ability to do it.

And then my burst was over and I sank into the familiarity of self-pity, such a comforting cocoon. The ringing of the phone broke my reverie. It was Ruth. She had to go to a meeting because she was so upset. Would I go? I agreed.

Without putting away my dissertational things, I began to get myself together. I didn't want Ruth to know I had been drinking, so I fixed some food and then took a cold shower. Then I made coffee and had two cups of it.

By the time Ruth arrived, I was completely sober.

I got into her car and looked at her. She was again very nervous and seemed ready to jump out of her skin.

"Anything special happening?" I asked.

Our whole ride was taken up by the recitation of her family problems. They were complicated. I began to see my being alone as a plus.

The meeting was a good meeting. I felt at ease and began to think about my problem. It really was not too difficult, was it? Just stop drinking and then be happy.

Ruth chose to speak and she was talking about one of the twelve steps and how she was applying it. It was Step Four, the making of a searching and fearless moral inventory and she was telling how she could not do this. I remembered how I had done this the first time in AA. It took me months to do it and then I went out and got drunk. It was a very upsetting experience. I felt immoral and weak, and it also made me feel excessively guilty. It added to my already big bag of guilt.

Now I listened to Ruth. She was crying but no longer able to go on speaking. I touched her hand and, in moments, she was quiet. One of the men was telling how he did it and how he used his sponsor to be the other human being to whom he revealed the exact nature of his wrongs.

I began to wonder why I was feeling guilt and atonement for my physical disease. Was I so immoral that I had to make this searching and fearless moral inventory?

I knew that I wouldn't do it again. Not this second time around. It was not the way for me. I began to see that my problem was the lack of self-confidence, a lack of self-esteem. I didn't need the heaviness of all this moral atonement, not now anyway, not if I were going to stay sober.

The meeting was closed and Ruth said she'd like to stay for coffee. The men were very friendly, some too friendly. Ruth had talked about some intimate details of her life and the men seemed to have remembered those parts. I knew that I would never, could never, discuss certain aspects of my life. First of all, they were over and done. To carry the remembrance of them with me was just damn foolish.

"Are you glad to be back?" Jerry was asking me with sort of a I-told-you-so grin.

Play the game, Jean. "Oh, yes, very glad."

"It's the only way. And you let Ruthie help you. She's our special gal. Aren't you, Ruthie?" he called across the table.

Ruth was too busy with the activities of her job as secretary to answer. She seemed extremely distraught and I got up so that we could leave.

"Going so soon? Why do the gals always leave early?" Jerry asked, not expecting an answer.

Ruth came over to me and in unison we said our good nights.

In the car Ruth again began crying.

"Can I do something?" I asked her.

"No, I don't think so. Everything is such a mess and I hate talking about everything else."

"Why not forget all that business about a searching and fearless moral inventory? It's just not necessary. Grab hold of today and move onward and upward."

"But I must work this program. I've been stuck on the fourth and fifth steps for several months. I want to make it. Others say that I can't make it without doing all of the steps."

I began to see how much I was questioning the steps. It was never so apparent to me as right now. Years ago I also saw how these two steps upset most women. Like everything else, if I didn't like something, I just left it. That's what I had done with the steps. Maybe that would keep me from real, lasting sobriety. But how could something so upsetting keep me sober?

"Here, move over and let me drive," I said to Ruth. She was still crying but not as much.

I didn't talk on the drive home. I was concerned about myself and how I would handle the AA program again. I wondered if I were sober now forever. I knew I wasn't. I wanted to be but my head was in too much of a turmoil. My body ached for a drink. Every night I got the shakes and a splitting headache. I had one now. I looked at the clock and saw that I could still make the liquor store if Ruth left right away.

I pulled into the dimly lit driveway and said good night. "And don't bother with all that stuff that's in the past, Ruth. Give today a chance. Give yourself a chance. O.K.?"

She mumbled something and then drove away.

I got into my car the minute she was out of the driveway and went to the liquor store. It was closed! Damn. I felt panic again. No liquor, nothing to drink. How could that be? What would I do? My heart was beating very hard and fast.

I drove the few blocks to my parents' home. The house was aglow. They always liked lots of light. Funny, I had forgotten that. My memories always seemed dark.

I let myself in with my key. My dad was watching TV and was very surprised.

"Hi, honey. Where have you been?" he asked, really concerned. My mother came into the room, walking quickly and lightly.

"Where have you been? Daddy and I have been wondering. How do you feel? Weren't you in the hospital for a few days?" she asked, not really waiting for an answer. "Last week we went to Lou and Ray's and tomorrow we are going to Philadelphia with them and then to dinner and then we'll come home to play cards." She stopped talking for a second. "Pete, did you make those arrangements? You know how Ray is about doing it."

She left the room, on the way to some more concern with trivia.

My dad's expression was one of resignation. Much lay between us that was unspoken.

"Want a drink, Dad? I'm going to get one."

"Sure. Scotch on the rocks."

The TV was filling the spaces of sound that my mother had left floating free.

I got the drinks quickly. After pouring a heavy drink in a glass for myself, I upended the bottle and took a big gulp from it. The liquor burned all the way down and it made me feel good, even though my eyes were smarting.

I carried the drinks into the living room and gave Dad his.

"Turn off the TV so we can talk."

"Weren't you watching a story?"

"It doesn't make any difference. Turn it off."

I crossed the room and turned it off.

"How have you been feeling?" he asked, genuinely interested. He carefully avoided talking about not seeing me in the hospital. Maybe he wasn't even aware of it. But I really knew he was. It wasn't his fault probably.

"I'm O.K. They found a sluggish gall bladder and that's not so bad. I have to be careful of what I eat."

"Doesn't drinking bother it?"

He zeroed right in on it. He knew why I was in the hospital. Maybe not all the details. But he knew.

"Well, it's not the best thing for it. But I haven't been drinking, so I don't know what would happen."

"How's your job?"

"O.K. Looks like our contract will be canceled."

"What will you do then? Better start looking now."

"Well, I took those courses at Lehigh to get into being an academic dean of a woman's college."

"But you're not trained to do that."

"Why not? I have enough education to do it," I said heatedly and defensively.

"You can't do it. Why don't you teach English in junior high school or something like that?"

My dad's being on the school board for twenty years made him believe he was an authority on the entire educational system in the country.

"Why should I teach junior high school with a Ph.D.?" My anger was rising.

"You don't have it yet. And you can't do anything else."

I threw down the rest of my drink, almost choking because I couldn't swallow it fast enough. Then I got up to leave.

"Why must you go so soon? You just came."

"I have a big day tomorrow. Say good-bye to Mother."

"Why don't you call her?"

I went to the stairway. "So long, Mother."

" 'Bye, honey. Be good."

The words echoed in my ear. I let out a big sigh, relieved to get away. It was always the same. Not one of us liked the other nor were we concerned about each other.

As I drove home, I felt the chill of the autumn air. My thoughts and emotions were in turmoil. I wanted to tear something apart, the rage in me was so strong. Thinking about the conversation with my parents made me see that I always turned to some form of self-destruction after our encounters. It continued to amaze me that, as an only offspring, I was always made to feel as if I didn't belong. There were many times when as a child I felt certain that I was adopted. But perhaps I demanded too much attention and love, affection and concern?

I was driving too fast for in-town driving. My tires squealed as I took a corner too fast and too short, yet the violent action somehow helped to release the destructive emotion.

There was no sense in taunting myself with thinking about drinking, since the liquor store was closed. Pennsylvania saw to controlled prices and in regulated hours.

The house was dark and made me feel lonely but there was nothing else to do but put the car in the barn and go to bed.

As I opened the door, I seemed overwhelmed with a lost feeling, wondering what it was all about. What are we here for? Why? It seemed such a futile experience.

My body was screaming for a drink. The four or five ounces I had had with my dad were just enough to set off the craving. My thoughts were consumed with the desire, as was my body.

I watched some TV but felt too restless to remain seated so I found some tranquilizers and took four to ensure some sleep.

Chapter 7

Ten days, ten whole days. Not a drink in that entire time. Oh, it was good to be sober and alert and almost happy. If only I could get over the obsession with the thought of it! Maybe never. But every minute of every day I thought about drinking. Time hung heavy, even though my job still required much driving and I had a new class at Lehigh. Doing research or reading or writing or driving or shopping or cleaning or dressing or beginning my new pastime of watching Nature, I thought always about drinking. My body still wanted to have a drink, to feel that warmth and to feel that nice easy feeling inside, to calm the shaking hands every now and then and to have that confidence. And to overcome the depression I now found myself falling into, every other day or so, the nagging feeling that someone or something was following me, and the feeling that there was nothing left in life. I began to think it must have been an alcoholic who coined the phrase "beside myself." That explained how I felt.

Although I had gone to AA with Ruth twice, I continued to search for more. The meetings just did not meet my needs. I began to read the work of Dr. Roger Williams from the University of Texas and found his vitamin theories very interesting. Dr. Williams based his theories on a metabolic imbalance and he believed an alcoholic could correct the condition with heavy doses of a certain vitamin formula plus glutamine. Dr. Williams writes, "In some alcoholics, remarkable responses have been obtained from using glutamine alone as a nutritional supplement. . . . It has been compared with its chemical relatives glutamic acid, asparagin, and the simpler amino acid glycine. These other substances had no effect whatever, but glutamine consistently decreased alcohol consumption [in rats]."

It took me weeks to get some glutamine and the special vitamin formula. It required writing to a laboratory in Texas, which I did. And I began taking it at once. So thrilled was I with it that I took it to AA to share my new knowledge but I was promptly stifled.

"But I simply want to share with all of you a way to get over some of the shakes and to *feel* better!"

It was to no avail. My suggestions that anyone take vitamins to help with his recovery was entirely taboo. I was angry and I felt rejected. It also seemed to be singularly closed-minded.

But I went on taking my glutamine, *believing* it was helping me. Ruth asked for some and she began taking it but said, "Please don't tell them at AA that I'm taking it. I'm also taking some medication from my doctor that I don't dare talk about."

It was all preposterous to me. This was not the way AA was when I first attended years ago. I wondered if it was what was intended by Bill W. No pills from a physician for high blood pressure? No chemicals? Yet the coffee consumed at each meeting was a chemical.

I decided to give up AA, although I would help Ruth when I could. She began to rely on me and I found that my talking to her helped me. But the meetings were a big aggravation. The men were set in their ways and ideas, they dominated the meetings, their stories were often lurid and contained an ego element of bragging, their descriptions of women were very often chauvinistic, which they carried with them into sobriety, and their constantly calling me a "gal" began to grate on my nerves. I found that with every meeting I attended, I had a greater desire to go out and get drunk. My attitude was "I'll show you, you poor dumb bastards."

But I had my ten days, although I felt myself slipping. I

knew I was going to drink, it was simply a matter of time. I used the psychological game of knowing that I could drink anytime and that all the liquor in the world was right there in a store just a few blocks from me and I'd get it when I wanted it. So what's so great about drinking? Who needs it? My decision was mine. Maybe I'd drink and maybe I wouldn't.

The winter months were bad. Sylvia came and said a quick good-bye. I envied her going to Florida and I was very sad after she left. More than that, I began to see some of the reason she gave for leaving. I had completely depended on her to get me out of every jam I got into. With her gone, I became afraid to drink, for I knew no one else was about to put up with my antics. They had had enough years ago—many, many years ago.

My ten days stretched into a month and I began to work on my dissertation. I was writing, to my great surprise and joy. It was even beginning to go rather well. I was extremely pleased with myself and the wonderful feeling of being just like everyone else, having it all together. I worked hard at work, even though it was menial work. The proposal had fallen through so I didn't have to go to Washington and work with Dick. But after each day of work, I hurried home, ate, and got right to my dissertation. It was really thrilling to feel that sense of accomplishment and doing.

It was just an ordinary day in midwinter that the day at Stratford turned the world around for me. As I entered the office I heard the news. Contract canceled. We were all finished! Right away, no month's notice or anything like that. Today's paycheck held the severance pay.

I could hardly accept it. Although I hated the job and knew what I was doing was not worth one third of what I was paid, it was still hard to grasp that as of today I would never be coming back here. Nor would I have money for the mortgage or my car or anything else, for that matter.

Everyone spent that Friday morning cleaning out desks. I did the same. Changes. Always changes. They threw me. While I cleaned my desk I had an utterly wild feeling, that nothing is dependable and that anything supportive is never to be trusted.

I couldn't wait to get away, to run away to anywhere, to get in my station wagon and just go, maybe to Florida, maybe to California, anywhere where I wouldn't see anyone I knew. Somehow I felt ashamed of myself, as if I had failed. Maybe if I had worked harder, this wouldn't have happened to the company! It sounded ridiculous, yet I felt guilty about all the times that I had skipped work and had been elsewhere.

I said my good-byes to the men. It was a sad parting, for we had worked well together.

As I walked to the parking lot with my boxes of stuff, I decided to go to the liquor store right next to the office. Boldly I walked into it, not caring who saw me now. I almost did it defiantly. I *did* do it defiantly. I'd show them! Damn company, damn everybody.

As was my usual custom, I opened the bottle, had a long swig, and then propped it on the seat next to me, with the whole of the bottle leaning against the right side of my body.

The drive home was easy, despite Friday traffic. I felt exhilarated, ready to take on anything. Who the hell needs that screwy company anyway? I knew that a frightening statistic I had read last week didn't apply to me. Wasn't it that 95 per cent of all persons losing a job after forty-five never again have full-time employment? Baloney. Here I was with my Ph.D. coming up and I didn't look forty-five to begin with, or so I convinced myself.

I broke into song intermittently as I drove. It really was a wonderful day. I felt released and exuberant. Why had I stopped drinking? It was obvious to me that I had been fooled into believing I had to give it up forever. Rot. And how could anything that made me feel so good be so bad?

When I got to Quakertown, I fell into an old pattern of visiting everyone I knew who drank. I spent the evening bragging, complaining, analyzing, self-pitying, boasting, monopolizing, and making a general fool of myself. It wasn't hard to do.

I awoke sometime in the middle of the night. It was my bedroom all right and the lights were on. My clothes were all twisted and wet. I was frightened and was trying to scream but nothing came out of my mouth. I couldn't make a sound. Nausea was my only feeling for the moment. I tried to run to the john but couldn't make it. Falling in the hallway, I was sick. And then I fell asleep in a huddle on the floor, stuporous and mercifully released from the regurgitating.

I spent the entire day on the couch, trying to recover and asking myself the big question. As I went over everything in my mind, I saw again the pattern of rejection stand out very clearly. All the negative feelings of no one wants me, etc., were apparent and so, too, was my automatic response. It was clear that all this came from no real belief in myself, no sense of value in my person.

The day was long. I wanted to go buy more liquor but I didn't. I sweated, shook, managed the fear by having the radio and TV on, both at the same time. I forced the dark, foreboding thoughts from my mind. I got out my book of Emerson and read a little bit of it. "How calmly and genially the mind apprehends one after another the laws of physics! What noble emotions dilate the mortal as he enters the councils of the creation, and feels by knowledge the privilege to BE!"

I put the book aside for a moment and looked at the golden light of October, that special quality of yellow-gold never to be seen in any other month. The sense of being a part of the whole, an identification with everything else, began to be a part of my feelings.

I picked up the book and read on. "Man's insight refines him. The beauty of nature shines in his own breast. Man is greater that he can see this, and the universe less, because Time and Space relations vanish as laws are known."

The magnitude of the thought overpowered me. My pettiness and my little world of "I" shriveled into the smallness it was.

I arose from the couch, turned off the TV and radio, and went outdoors to walk, something I hadn't done for decades.

I walked around the yard and began to look at each bush. Then I felt the leaves and branches. The touch was strange to my fingers, yet it was thrilling to think about all of us as a part of the same whole, that we were simply different sides of the same coin.

My lesson in Nature was interrupted by my splitting headache and having to go to the house for aspirin.

The ravages of the drinking were getting to me and I went to
bed without any more mind-stretching. The exhaustion that
came from the drinking was greater than my curiosity for a solution to life.

Awaking Saturday, I realized that I no longer had to worry
about getting to the office on Monday morning. No longer
would I have to worry about trying not to drink too much on
Sunday night. But I also knew I had to begin looking for a job
right away. What? Where? My dissertation was almost ready
to turn in and then I would be able to get something without
any trouble at all.

It was a great Saturday morning until Mother called to say
Daddy was in the hospital. He had been taken yesterday, after
a heart attack. Yesterday!

I drove over to my home and got my mother to go to the
hospital. It took only a few minutes.

My dad looked very pale although he was cheerful.

"Hi, honey."

"Hello, Dad. What happened?"

"Here, Pete. I brought your slippers, and your robe, and the
newspaper and your mail," Mother was saying, all the while
putting things away in a flurry.

"Not much. Just got a pain," my dad answered. "Oh, stop
putting all that stuff here. I didn't want it now," he said to my
mother.

"But you'll need it and then you'll have it," she said.

"But I'm not *supposed* to have any of it."

We all sat uncomfortably. I decided to leave, because every
time I looked at my father I felt my throat tighten and I had
to stop the tears.

"I've got some errands to do and I'll be back in an hour,
Mother. So long, Dad."

I kissed him lightly. Why couldn't I say all the things I
felt? Why couldn't I tell him that I needed him, that I wanted
to tell him I loved him, that I cared what happened, that I
wasn't told he was here?

"See you later."

I left quickly, crying silently, feeling as if my heart were bursting from pressure.

I got into my car in the parking lot and drove to the liquor store. I started to go in but turned around and went back to the car. Sitting behind the wheel, I waited a minute and then decided to get a half pint. I got out of the car and went in to get it. I was about to turn around when the clerk was there, asking me what I wanted. I got a half pint.

Walking out of the store, I felt it very carefully. The feel of the bottle was strange.

I drove home very fast, as if I were being chased. And I was. My head buzzed with accusations of others, with curses for events, with resentment and rejection, with unexpressed love for my father, with bitterness for life, with sadness for what was happening over which I had no control. Since events didn't change, I knew I had to.

I opened the bottle and smelled it. I hated the smell but I knew how great it would feel when I drank. In a burst of rage, I threw the bottle to the floor with such a force that the glass was shattered into thousands of splinters. I left the room. It reeked with the smell of liquor.

I had to get my life together. I had to get me together. Just then the phone rang and it was Ruth.

"Can you help me? Do you have a minute to talk?"

"Sure. Would you like to come over?"

"No, I'd just like to talk. Everything is going wrong in my family. My husband lost his job, my oldest daughter is pregnant, and my son just got caught in an accident and had some marijuana on him." She was crying.

I let her cry for a few seconds.

"It's all very bad but, since you can't change the things that have happened, you must change you. Isn't that right?"

I was surprised at my wisdom, at the iteration of all that I had thought just a short time ago.

"Yes, you're right. I never thought of it that way."

"Not only that, but a drink never makes any problem better, does it?" I was silent while this sank in. "And you are very capable of doing what you must do. You are the only strong one left, so don't lose your head."

"I'm so glad I called, because I know what to do now." She hesitated a moment. "You're so good to take time to talk to me. I know you have problems of your own but it never seems so. You have so much confidence."

Brother, she should know! "Thanks, Ruth."

I hung up and stood looking out the window. Everyone is weak but not everyone shows it. By believing strength and confidence, one can eventually live it, because it becomes a cloak. The important thing to remember is that everyone is unsure and uncertain, faced with new problems to which there are no *seeming* solutions.

I drove to the hospital to get my mother. I wanted to talk to my dad but he was asleep. I was disappointed.

Taking Mother home, I was silent most of the drive. She did the talking and I listened not at all carefully. My mind was planning what to do with the rest of my life. My dissertation must be finished within the week and delivered to the University of Pennsylvania and then I would get a job. Meanwhile a friend from New England was asking me to go to Maine with her. I wanted to go but didn't see how I could manage it.

"So long, Mother." I had stopped in front of the house.

"And I said I'd be back tonight."

"O.K., I'll be here for you."

The next few weeks were a maze of hospital visits and, for me, unsuccessful interviews for a job. I had sent out fifty resumés and, from those, I had two interviews, both of which fell through after the appointments.

It was very frightening. The statistic I had read about my chances on new employment seemed to be proving right. I began to live on the edge of panic, because I was living on borrowed money. My unemployment checks were almost at an end and that meant there would be no income whatever.

Out of this period of misery came word that my dissertation was accepted and I was now a Ph.D. It was hard to get used to at first, since it had been so long in coming. But it made no difference in my getting a job, because my age was against me.

That too was hard for me to adjust to. Too old! It seemed that I was just beginning to live. My drinking was well in hand. Sometimes two weeks went by. Right now it was over three weeks since I had had a drink. The last time had been when Ann and I went to Philadelphia to take my dissertation to the university. We stopped for lunch and that's where it all began with three cocktails and then three more in another cocktail lounge, ending with our buying a case of champagne, of which I drank two bottles. The old nightmare took over and several days passed before I was able to do anything. It took several more to get over the depression.

My dad was recuperating nicely and I visited him almost every day but old tensions were always present. He was proud of my new degree and my obvious attempts not to drink. But we never talked of it. Only the trivia of life was worthy of conversation. However, I managed to tell him that I was thinking about going to Maine to look for a job and then rent my house.

"Why not stay here and see things through? It would be easier to get a job in the area you're familiar with than somewhere else. Don't you think?" he asked.

"No, I don't think." My mind was made up and I really wasn't listening to him. Rarely had I ever but, then, when did I ever listen to anyone? Strong-willed, everyone said. Stubborn.

Yes, I was all of those things. And more. It suddenly occurred to me that I really wasn't a very nice person. The thought shocked me. My belief was always that everyone would like me but now I knew that that was not necessarily true.

"What will you do with the house?" he asked logically.

"I'm going to rent it furnished. That will pay the bills."

"You're making a big mistake," he said with firmness.

"No, I'm not." The impasse, one will butted against the other. Time to leave. I stood up.

"See you tomorrow."

"Won't you stay for dinner?"

"No, Florence is coming from Rhode Island for a few days. But, if I go to Maine, we'll drive there together and I'll look for a job."

He refrained from more comments.

"Tell Mother I said 'hello' when she gets home from her party."

I left, feeling very sad and depressed. It wasn't right for me to go now, but I knew I was going.

Florence arrived on the next Wednesday, and by Saturday I had begun to empty the house of its contents. The ten years I had lived in it were counted in collections of little value other than personal memories. It seemed as if a large phase of my life had just ended. The curtain had fallen and I was in a new compartment, this time without a bottle for comfort.

Although I wasn't drinking, I still thought only about drinking, and staying sober was a constant battle. I was not happy nor was I contented. The furies raged in me and I was hard put to keep them under control. Maine represented a new life, a way to run from this old one. In addition to the furies being with me always, I was also very depressed most of the time. The sadness of all life seemed to pervade my being. So much was missing for me. Removal of liquor merely made me see my deficiencies, made me see I had few coping mechanisms other than drinking, which wasn't coping at all.

The worst part was the never being without the thought of the urge to drink. I had to overcome it, that was the way to be without these bouts of drinking, which now replaced the everyday drinking. A trip to Maine should take care of it, since Florence knew my drinking problem but also knew of my ending it. Essentially this was part of the trip, no drinking for me. I began to feel the cage but wanting to go overpowered my misgivings.

I said good-byes to my parents and we left for Maine, my house still unrented.

It was February and we drove leisurely. The Maine coast was lovely in the starkness of winter light. As long as I pushed my problems from my mind, I was able to enjoy the beautiful days of water and rocks.

After several attempts at finding a place, suddenly we met with good fortune and were able to rent a cottage right on the water's edge for very little money. It was winterized and it had three bedrooms and several other large rooms. It was most comfortable, the best part being that it was on the water's edge.

And then I prepared to be happy, but that wasn't the case. My restlessness was ever upon me. I walked the edge of the water, studying the sea gulls, listening to the lap of time in each wave.

I began looking for a job in Portland but found closed doors. Maine was a depressed area and there were no jobs and nothing anywhere close to what I could do.

I got into the habit of driving into Biddeford, the small town closest to our cottage, for the mail and then buying six cans of beer. Sometimes I'd buy wine, but it was very difficult concealing it from Florence, although I was able to get away with not always being detected. On several occasions I got drunk and fought through the hell of recovery and depression.

But the depression lingered. It was time to get to work on myself again and I went to the Biddeford library for as many books as I could find about life and ways to live it. Florence was interested in the occult and I began to read about psychic experiences and life after death. I found it very interesting and it opened a world I never knew was there, but I had many reservations about psychic experiences.

Each afternoon I would lie on the bed for an hour and concentrate on deep, even breathing, thinking about space and permitting myself to be divorced from my body. One time I did see the white light at the top of my head, but only once. Although there seemed to be some evidence of those here on earth speaking to others, I always found a certain reticence in myself in believing all of it wholeheartedly.

My best times were spent walking along the beach and sitting on a rock, trying to find some answers. My Emerson was with me always and I clung to paragraphs to mull over while sitting before the pounding waves.

One afternoon, in the bright winter light of Maine, I took my book and climbed onto a rock, conscious ever of the smell of the air, the sound of the water, and the stillness of every moment. It reminded me of the time I was at the Grand Canyon and everyone was whispering. I knew I couldn't speak aloud now, too overpowering was Nature.

I had begun to think much about God and my relation to Him. Reading Emerson and learning of his deep faith began to force me to re-examine my lackluster beliefs. I knew I believed in God but that's where it all ended for me. All I could remember from church was a minister gesturing heavenward, as if God were there above us. Emerson's concept thoroughly confused me, yet through the study of Nature, I began to have a real feeling for the place in which I lived. My relation to it began to have a meaning for me and I was eager to learn more. I began to realize, ever so slowly, that I had no delineation of myself, had no clear beliefs, had no philosophy or religion. How could I have bumbled along for so many years in this state of ignorance?

I opened my Modern Library volume of Emerson and read, "Nature looks provokingly stable and secular, but it has a cause like all the rest; and when once I comprehend that, will these fields stretch so immovably wide, these leaves hang so individually considerable? Permanence is a word of degrees. Everything is medial. Moons are no more bounds to spiritual power than bat-balls."

It goes on, "The key to every man is his thought. Sturdy and defying though he look, he has a helm which he obeys, which is the idea after which all his facts are classified. He can only be reformed by showing him a new idea which commands his own."

Yes, a new idea. That was the entire answer for me. I had had no new ideas for many years, and, if I had, I did not permit them to affect me.

The shallowness of my life appalled me. How could anyone of seeming intellectual capacity be so completely removed from meaningful personal thinking? It was as if my mind had been separated from my emotions, trained in excess, while my emotions stayed locked into infantilism by my expertise in running away by using liquor.

It was growing more dark than light. I looked out across the vastness of the ocean and a thrill of being alive claimed me and

I felt a great hope about myself and what I could do. It would take much work but I wanted to overcome my shortcomings, I wanted to be worthy as a person, I wanted happiness and peace.

In that brief moment I knew I could have all those things. I felt a great urge to put on paper the feelings I was experiencing in these days of a new beginning.

I walked along the beach for a short while in the fading light and felt one with all Nature. I looked at all the living things at the water's edge and felt kinship. The sea gulls had new beauty and I wanted to embrace them. I was bursting with the joy and beauty of the moment. Breathing deeply, I broke into a trot and ran as long as I could before being utterly exhausted.

Turning back, I tried catching my breath, gulping mouthfuls of sea air. I hurried back to the cottage to tell Florence.

That night we talked at length about the beauty of the sea. After Florence went to bed, I looked into the blackness of the night and saw a ship that was rather close. Its many lights made it look like a passing Christmas tree. The moon was full and it was a spectacular sight.

Finally I went to bed and took the four meprobamate I had become accustomed to taking for sleep.

So alive was my mind that I awakened before dawn. I had wanted to watch everything that took place in relation to the ocean. Two bright stars, one far above the other, twinkled above the flat, gray ocean. It was a time to know perfect Oneness, and I did, in that briefest space of silent time.

But then came a time of realization of bills and money and life . . . real life, the one I had spent all my waking time running away from. It became necessary for me to apply for jobs and I began the process of going into Portland and trying my luck once again.

Florence continued to say to me, "You must not be discouraged. Something will turn up. Let me speak to Mrs. Bailey."

She was the woman realtor we lived next to and she had been extremely helpful to us in everything else. Florence did speak to her and she gave me the name of a woman in Portland who was in some social service. I had an appointment with her, but that also proved fruitless.

I knew I had to consider going home. My house had not been rented, yet the mortgage payments went on, as did my car payments, as did my living expenses in Maine, which, surprisingly, were minimal. My real expenses came from the responsibilities at home.

Then I received a letter from Mother saying that Father was again in the hospital.

That morning, after reading the mail, I went to a grocery store and bought a quart of wine. Driving along the Maine coast, I drank it and went back to town to the liquor store for a fifth of vodka. I worked on that for a short while before going back to face Florence and the inevitable argument. When would I ever be able to do exactly what I wanted to do in life without feeling defensive or guilty?

I went back to the cottage and we had a frightful scene. I spent the remainder of the day with my bottle and, by evening, I was overcome with the feeling of uselessness and depression. Everything in my world was gone and everything was finished.

When I awoke, it was morning. I was in a place I didn't recognize but Florence was beside me.

"What happened?" I asked her. Her face registered worry and concern.

"You took an overdose of pills. The ambulance brought you here."

My mind refused the information. Sleep was better.

When I next woke, the hospital was quiet and I knew it was night. Then I began to go over everything. I remembered drinking most of the day but I had no recollection whatever of anything past late afternoon. A blackout. That was always bad news.

I was overwhelmed with depression. Why hadn't I really done it this time? What was the use of living? Nothing, *nothing*, was worth it.

Just then a man walked into the room. In the dim light I could barely see him.

"Good evening. I'm Pastor Smythe from the Methodist church in Saco." He bent over me as he was talking.

"Good evening." I couldn't speak. It was all I could do to keep from crying, so glad was I to be with another human being. It was as if I had been cut off from the human race for eons.

He patted the top of my hand as it lay on the bed cover.

"How are you feeling?"

"I guess all right." Something kept me from telling him how I really felt, but I wanted to. I wanted to ask him for the answers. How do I find God? How does He find me?

"Perhaps you'll come to my church when you leave here. What is your church?"

"I've just moved here from Pennsylvania. I'm a Lutheran."

"I had a parish in Pennsylvania, at Pottstown. Do you know where it is?"

I felt as if I had met someone from home. "Why that's only fifteen miles from Quakertown!"

"Just around the corner. I came to know many Pennsylvania Dutch, as they are called. Do you know them?"

"I should guess so. I am one!"

"But I thought . . ." His voice trailed off in confusion.

"You thought everyone wears the clothing of the Amish?"

"Yes."

"Actually, anyone of German extraction and whose forebears settled in Pennsylvania is called Pennsylvania Dutch. My dad went to school where only Pennsylvania Dutch was spoken."

"Do you speak it?"

"No. I've always hated being known as that. It seemed degraded and backward to me."

"Why it's no such thing," he protested.

For a moment he hesitated. "Would you like me to say a prayer for you before I leave?"

"Yes."

Standing by the bed, he bowed his head and said a very short prayer. All the while I wondered if he knew why I was in the hospital. I thought he did, since he never once asked me if I had had an operation or what I was there for. A flush of shame passed over me.

"Amen," he finished.

He looked at me directly; I could see the sincerity in his face. He was truly believing. I envied him.

"Let me see you in church."

"You might," I said as he was leaving.

Brief though the meeting was, his words and his presence stayed within my thoughts much of the time I was in the hospital. I spoke to almost no one because of the shame I felt, yet the attitude of the nurses in Maine was quite different from the attitude I encountered with the nurses in Pennsylvania, where they had only derision for attempted suicides. It simply was not the case here. I was treated with compassion and I appreciated it. I had not a shred of self-esteem left. I felt only loathing and disgust for myself. No longer did I feel much self-pity. I knew that I had made a real mess of everything and I knew that everything I did was cowardly and characterless. I began to see through the fog that I surrounded myself with. Those days beside the edge of the ocean had not been misspent nor were my hours with Emerson. It became exceptionally clear to me just exactly what I had to do: pick myself up, dust myself off, make a new Jean, and grab a hold on life.

There, see how easy it is? Nothing to it! Everybody out there does it every day. Why should you be different?

Florence came and my reverie was interrupted.

"Well, you're looking better." She smiled, although she still looked very tired from the ordeal I had put her through.

"I do feel better. I see you brought my clothes. I'm all set to go," I said with some real animation.

"You look—ready to leave."

"I am."

Then I told her about the minister's visit and that I wanted to go to church on Sunday. Florence always liked going to church.

"That sounds good. I'd like to go."

She handed me my clothes and I started to dress.

"You'd better wait for the discharge. The doctor must see you. What's he like?"

"He's very nice," and, just as I was saying that, Dr. Johnson came in. He was a big hulk of a man, unemotional in his dealings with me and I wondered if he were that way with all his patients.

"You seem ready to go home. Are you?"

"Yes." I knew there was another question lurking. "I'm ready to get with it."

"Good." He smiled. "You can dress now. I'll see that the discharge is processed. Come see me in a few days."

"O.K.," I said lightly. I knew I wouldn't. I had already closed the door on this chapter and was ready to get on with the search for a soul.

He was gone and I dressed hurriedly, eager to get away and back to the ocean. I was still weak and very light-headed.

"Let me help you," Florence offered. She did.

"I guess I have everything. At least a woman doesn't have much baggage coming in the way I did," I tried joking unsuccessfully.

Florence was very silent. I could see she was upset and wanted to talk about something.

"You're angry?"

"That's not the right word. I don't want to talk about it now," she said.

We left the hospital and drove the short distance to the cottage, perhaps ten miles.

No sooner in the door, Florence began to speak. "I'm sorry you have been through this experience but I must tell you that I can't go through it again. You must promise that it won't happen again, that you won't drink again."

I felt very sorry for her and what I had put her through, yet I couldn't promise anything. I *wanted* to promise but couldn't. Anyway, we had to go home. All my problems and concerns were in Pennsylvania. I felt very guilty being here in Maine and being so close to inner peace while walking along the ocean.

"I'm sorry about everything. We'll go home. I must. Maybe you'd like to stay here for a while. There is still some rent."

"No, I'll go along too."

I never knew if she went along because of worrying about me, but I suspect that that was the real truth. My life had always been filled with persons who really cared and I rarely thought about it. Despite all I put my friends through, almost all remained friends. I began to think about that hard. I tried to recall what most of them said but it was fuzzy. My recall about almost everyone in my life was of loyalty and love toward me. What did they see that I didn't?

"I'll begin packing. Why don't you lie down and rest for a while? Then we'll walk along the beach."

"O.K."

Lying on the couch, I became conscious of the ocean's steady pounding on the beach. It was a thrilling sound, as if one were privileged to sit in on the noise of eternity. I listened intently, for this memory would have to serve me well. Strange how now I wanted to collect memories, yet the memories I already had I knew I must put aside and not ever spend life reacting to them. I had to grab for the now. It became imperative that I live to the fullest.

Great thoughts. Just simply not great enough to dispel the threatening depression that began to settle over me.

Florence came into the room. She looked sad and very tired. Small wonder. Why was I never before conscious of what I put others through? I could honestly say that I never *really* thought about it.

The emergence of this dark and uncaring side of my personality shocked me. But then, what was one more shock these days?

"Shall we go for a walk?"

"Yes." I got off the couch and we left the cottage.

It was toward dusk. We walked silently. The air was salty and invigorating. It was just the right temperature. Little creatures scuttled over the beach as we walked, seeking a new home after being disturbed by us. There was a ship in the distance and sea gulls everywhere. Again the pounding of the surf impressed upon my brain a truth I rarely kept company with. I wanted to keep it all, forever and longer, but it was all about to be erased by the reality of home-going. I dreaded going home to face all the real problems of my life. Every area was in chaos but most especially my inability to find a job. What was I going to do? I began to feel real panic and succumbed to it.

"It's beautiful, isn't it?"

So carried away was I by my problems that I let the moment slip by. And I saw that that was a big failure of mine, never enjoying the moment I was in, always in one past or dreaming of one to come.

"I don't want to go home!" I declared.

I looked at Florence and realized that she also didn't want to go home. I resented my father's illness and that I was an only daughter, only child. I resented having to worry about money, not having it and needing it. There was a time when I didn't have to worry about money, when my parents always kept me supplied with more than I ever needed. But from the time of my almost year in the hospital with daily psychiatric treatment and the months afterward as an outpatient in a city apartment, my father's nest egg had slowly but irreversibly dwindled.

It was galling and aggravating and unchangeable. Damn, damn, damn. I kicked the sand and it flew up in a cloud of thin gravel spray.

"What's wrong?" Florence asked reasonably.

I was angry. I could feel my eyes flashing. "Everything. The whole damned world. I hate it and everyone in it."

I stalked off, walking, half-running, away from her and along the water's edge. Minutes later she caught up with me.

"It will all work out. You must believe that everything will be right if you see it that way. Why not read Unity?"

For months, Florence had been wanting me to read Unity, but it all sounded like pie in the sky and I had refused to have anything to do with it.

"Why must you keep insisting that I read something I don't want to?" I asked irritably.

"Because I know it will help you a very great deal. It's not at all what you think."

"Well I won't read it."

The childishness came through to me. You ignoramus!

I turned and walked back to the cottage, Florence walking silently next to me. I had ruined our last walk along the beach with my quick rage and quick tongue. Would I ever learn how to control both? Would I ever learn anything about myself? I seemed to know about myself, but could I correct those things I had learned?

We went into the cottage and I began to pack. I noticed that Florence was already ready to leave. Life, a great big bowl of sour cherries.

After Florence went to bed, I sat in the living room for a long time, trying to find answers while listening to the lap of water, the undulating waves of time present.

As I thought about the ocean I played with the tantalizing idea that the ocean stays, only I leave. The ocean and everything else in Nature is here for what we call forever, yet all of us on the human side come and go. We are the passers-by, we are the transients, the gypsies. We are the strangers, the whispers of life that waft across the earth's surface.

Time stays, man leaves.

I let out a long sigh, wondering how I could overcome the fear and anger I felt. And drinking, always the drinking. Which came first? The fear and anger that led me to drinking? Or the drinking that created the fear and anger? But what difference does it make, I wondered. I still had to overcome the drinking. It seemed that I was beginning to make some little progress. Now I had binge drinking, which was new to me. Before I had binge sobriety. At least I had reversed that. But how could I overcome the whole of it, give it up forever? Just the thought of "forever" terrorized me. There *must* be a way to be happy without drinking. Why did I drink? Certainly not to feel better, because it didn't make me feel better, only worse. I had even come to hate the person I became when drinking. That was new. I used to think that I became one of the earth's more interesting women. Now I could really see that that wasn't true. So why did I drink? Well, obviously, to run away. But from what? From me, sweet, little ole me? That's it, baby, you got it right this time. But why? Well, you're no damn good, you're a failure, you feel angry and guilty almost all the time, you're upset about all the people you've hurt and your crazy actions and unforgivable behavior, you're just a real bummer.

O.K., so that's where I begin. With myself.

I got a paper and pencil and, before sitting down again, I looked out into the blackness of the night and listened intently to the ocean's roar, an earful of eternity. Oh, to live by the side of the sea, to walk on the water's edge at any time of night or day!

Sometime, I promised myself.

With the paper and pencil, I drew a line down the center of the page. On the right side I put a plus mark and on the left side I placed a minus sign. Then I thought about me, the person called Jean. Quickly I filled the negative side of the columns. It was everything I'd been thinking about. But then I came to the positive side and that's where the problem began. What did I like about myself? Well . . . let's see . . . humor, yes, I have a sense of humor. What else? Well . . . let's see . . . ummm . . . I have . . . ah, I am . . . Oh nuts! I tore the sheet of paper in two and threw it across the room.

Again I became conscious of my childishness. Maybe that's where I should begin. Try to think and act like an adult. That would help.

So I decided to get to bed and get some sleep for the long drive home. Oh, how I hated to leave! All to go home and face problems.

Before leaving the room, I opened the door for a last moment of listening to the ominous roar of the ocean. There it was again, the enormity of its power, the universal strength.

I went off to bed but was unable to sleep. I tossed and turned most of the night, wrestling with thoughts of drinking. Oh, to have a drink! In recent months, it had become obvious to me that my drinking was used to run from any form of unpleasantness. That thought had never occurred to me before, during all the many years of heavy drinking. Realizing it now sort of spoiled drinking in a way. Guilt feelings assailed me before, during a drinking bout. My weaknesses as a human being, my immaturity had become all too evident in the past months of thinking my way out of a bottle. I knew that, once begun, some physical cycle was set in motion and I had no control over the results. That part had been made clear to me several thousand times over the past years.

Now, tossing in the darkness, I felt torn between wanting to be drunk and not drinking.

Problems! Decisions!

"Can't you sleep?" Florence asked.

I was startled. "No."

"I can't either."

She left the room and went to the living room. I joined her.

"Don't you think you could stay until the rent is finished this month?" she asked.

"I'd love to but I must get home. Maybe I can get things squared away. You know I'm borrowing money right now to be here."

"I know. Well, I'm packed."

"You go back to bed, I'll pack now."

Packing took very little time. It was dawn by the time I had begun. The early morning ocean sounds were already audible.

Chapter 8

Quakertown looked exactly the same as when I left it several months earlier. Only my father looked different. The end was written on his features and I was twisted and choked inside. I felt rage and hatred for all of life. My emotions were not to be trusted, so violent were they. Others must have sensed it, since most people left me alone.

I felt cheated. I wanted to talk to my dad, to tell him that I was really going to manage my problem, but he was just barely able to manage staying alive.

On the last Tuesday I sat with him during the afternoon while my mother attended a luncheon in his honor for the thirty years he had devoted to school directorship. I marveled at the irony of life, how we attend to the closing ceremonies and how they are planned to meet the exigencies of time. There was something macabre about all of it.

As we spent the afternoon together, I wondered how long it would be, this suffering, this living yet not living.

But I didn't have long to wait. On Saturday morning I was called home to help get him to the hospital again.

And that night the phone call came.

Tragedy is funny. You know it's happening to you but you don't react to it until you have time, maybe days later, after all the realities of social mores have been cared for.

On the day of the funeral, I took several large gulps of whiskey but it just wasn't the same, not after the long stretches of time I'd been knowing sobriety. It tasted like poison and I hated myself for trying to reawaken a craving I had almost tamed.

But I drank and the not taking more later was again a tremendous challenge. I knew that I could never drink like others and I was just about ready to accept the fact that I was indeed an alcoholic and had been most of my life, having shown classic signs of it at the age of eighteen.

"It's so nice you're home, Jean. Now you can look after your mother," Hilda Smith was saying; she had been a friend of our family's for decades, now here for the viewing.

"Yes, just in time," I said with genial acceptance. She should *know!* My mind was aflame with anger and resentment.

"How nice to see you, Jean. Your mother will certainly need you now," said another friend who came by.

"Oh, yes. Thank you for coming," I murmured. When would it end, this barbaric ritual for the dead?

"That's such good cake. Have you had some?" one of Mother's bridge-club women said. "I'll miss your father. He was such a good man, don't you think?"

Why answer? "Yes, he was," I said, hating her, watching her while she munched on her cake, plump fingers carrying it to her mouth.

"There you are, Jean. I've been looking for you. Too bad about your father. What are you going to do now, move in with your mother?"

Funny, I had never thought about it but the hand that writes on the wall was beginning to write something for me, and I didn't like what I was seeing. Move home? Never! Give up the farm? How could I? That's where I drank and recovered and wrote my dissertation, it was part of me, bringing it back from a ramshackle house to something livable. Move home? With Mother? Oh, for a drink! But that avenue was definitely shut and I wanted it shut. I wanted to be something new and not what I'd been. I wanted to be rid of the utter disgust I felt for myself as a person. In this past half year I had begun to get several glimpses of myself and I despised every one of them.

I disliked failure and I knew that I was a failure, not in the professional sense but as a human being. My perceptions of others, most especially myself, were clouded by my self-absorption. Now, this minute, in this room filled with humanity, I began to look at the people, to see them as persons with needs and desires. How did they go about satisfying them? Surely if these people could make it, I could too. What had I found so hard about making it? Did I simply give in and say I couldn't do it, not meet life's demands, life's problems? It seemed that way but how did it happen? Why did I walk away from everything?

"Your mother is taking this so well, isn't she?"

"Yes, she certainly is. Thank you for coming."

And now the present situation demanded action and clear thought without emotional reaction. Sell your furniture, rent or sell your house, move home, have the shoulder operation you've been putting off, get a job, and, if there is none, make one for yourself.

"So nice to see you, Jean. You got home just in time to help your mother."

"Yes," I murmured.

No emotional reactions. Just do it. And then get some kind of meaningful plan and a working philosophy. Everything you've used before must be scrapped.

"You're looking well, Jean."

She can see I don't have a hangover and I'm not drinking. *That's* what she really means. Whoops, Jean. There you go with that defensiveness. Believe that she means what she says and nothing more. O.K. Done.

"Thank you." I smiled. "I'm feeling a lot better than I have."

"So nice you're home. You'll be needed."

Needed? Does my mother need me? Needed. Hmmmmmm.

"Are you home to stay, Jean?"

"Yes, I guess so." Was I?

"Hope we'll be seeing you. It's been a long time since we've talked."

"Yes. See you."

I looked at Nancy carefully. She really seemed to want to talk to me. Could it be?

I looked at her again and found her gaze resting on me. I smiled and she smiled back.

How about that? Maybe it was true that what we express is what is returned to us. I decided to try it.

"Hello, Jim. Nice seeing you." I smiled broadly.

He smiled and took my hand. "Long time no see. You're looking great."

"So are you. How's your wife?"

He beamed. "She's over there. Wait, I'll get her."

"Fine."

While I waited I thought about this new key I had found. It seemed to be true. But then, hadn't I read somewhere that our first concern is ourself? And isn't that true?

Jim came back with his wife, June. We made small talk and all the while I observed that my extension of good feelings was reflected by them. We get back what we give. Give away your sobriety to keep it. My helping Ruth a few months ago had helped me. "Do unto others . . ."

I began to get restless. I wanted to be away from this evening and begin my life anew. I wished I could talk to my father about it but that phase was gone, a chapter closed. I knew I would always miss my dad and be sorry for what I never said or did. It would affect me to the degree I would let it and I knew, if I weren't careful, it could throw me if I thought too much about it. I had really bombed out with my dad. I was filled with regret and yet I soon learned its uselessness.

I crossed the room to my mother's side. She looked shriveled and tired. I took her arm and said, "I think we should get to bed. How about if I put things away?"

"All right, but I must talk to everyone."

"But you already have. We've seen them for hours."

Thank heaven everyone was leaving. I was glad for the heavy occasion to be over. I was done with my father's death. It was over. I was ready to move on.

Standing at the door, I said my good-byes to our friends, people I'd known all my life, people who meant nothing to me because I loathed small towns and those persons and conventions associated with them. I had made a mockery of everything that they stood for. No wonder I could sense their negative feelings for me, and yet many forgave me and even expressed concern for me.

"Good night. Thank you for coming."

They passed out the door, squeezing my hand and that of my mother as they went. My aunts and uncles stayed afterward but I disappeared as quickly as possible. I was free from the oppression of reality.

My friend Florence stayed and, after slipping away for a short period, we went back to Mother's house and prepared for the long night ahead.

My body and mind screamed for a drink. I almost yearned for the pain of something other than reality. The next two days I was thoroughly consumed with the problems of burial and taxes. Florence stayed at the farm while I stayed with my mother, who seemed to be in a total daze. One time, while looking out the kitchen window, she said, "He liked you so much. He often asked me to call you to come over but I knew you were busy."

A fist squeezed my heart into a pulp and I heard the ticking of my time bomb. That day I took my mother to sign the autopsy report. The military funeral was the next day.

I suppose the gray areas of life tend to fade away with the application of self-discipline and restraint, even though one thinks the long days of sadness will never end. Somehow we need to wallow in the event for a period, as if we must. The day after the funeral I drove past the cemetery and the men were filling in the grave. I felt totally disoriented and strange. For hours I drove around before returning to Mother's home.

She was totally distraught for many weeks following. Her life was completely interlocked with my father's and she was now left to wait out the rest of her life.

My days disappeared into weeks. I had rented an IBM composer and began with several jobs from the local printers. But work was very slow. Never was I able to make the amount of monthly rent, of $150.00. The future was very bleak. My thoughts began to turn to writing a monthly newsletter for retired persons. I also began to consider selling my property, for I knew I had to move home with my mother full-time. Florence returned to Rhode Island. Both Mother and I hated to see her go, for she had helped us immeasurably over the difficult period of transition.

On the day she left, I hit a low spot of almost unmanageable proportions. I had to face up to leaving my farm, my first real home.

Before going back to the farm, I drove around for a long time with no special place in mind. I drove as a means of keeping myself occupied to keep from drinking. I wondered how normal people handled all this time that stretches out so long? What to do with time? There was so much of it. I would certainly have to keep myself busy. But with what?

My life seemed to be very empty. No family except Mother, no children, no husband or relationship, no job, no money, no close friends who didn't drink, no hobbies, because there had never been time, and no hope of much in the future.

The bleakness of it all hit me hard. I began to perspire, just the way I always had when I thought about the dissertation. But you got that finished!

Unless I got some work soon, I'd lose my farm and Mother would lose her house. Then what?

I turned the car around sharply and gave the accelerator pedal a punch. The car sped away and I gloried in the surge of power. I wanted to drive wildly and scream and yell. Maybe drive into a wall. Everything inside me was rebelling . . . my mind, my body, my spirit. Why stop drinking? What the hell for? Who wants to be sober and miserable and face all this crap? What good is it? What does it accomplish? *Why* must we do it? Just because everyone else was doing it didn't make it the right way. And certainly most others didn't seem happy. That was for sure!

I drove to the liquor store and bought a pint of Seagram's. It felt good to stand in the brightly lighted store among my old friends, bottles of every color and hue and shape. They could be depended upon. Only my reaction to it could not. But that was all different now. Maybe.

Racing home, I dreamed about drinking and being completely relaxed and free from problems. It would be glorious.

But as I walked into the silent house, I knew that I probably wouldn't. I was scared. I didn't want to be sick and miserable and have to go through the drying out all over again. I forced myself to think about shaking apart, to think about heaving and vomiting, I thought about the terrible depression and the inconsolable sadness that went with it all.

I walked to the kitchen and tore open the bottle's seal. The glass was handy for me to fill with the liquor. I swirled it and looked at it carefully. I tantalized myself with it.

Where had I read something about an obsession with liquor as part of it? It was certainly true for me. I was obsessed with the thought of drinking and wanting to be drunk but not sick. I began to remember the days when I was hooked on pills as well, all kinds of pills. But mainly the amphetamines. Pills and booze. Booze and pills. It was a real wonder that I was still walking around. Then I never knew what I had taken or how much. But who cared? I know I didn't.

I began to see that my present feelings were different. I really cared now. That's real funny, Jean. Here you stand with a glass of liquor in your hand.

I poured it down the sink. Then poured the remainder of the bottle down the sink. I began to giggle . . . soon my sink would have cirrhosis. That makes two of us. Maybe we can go to AA together, my sink and I.

AA. What was I going to do? I hated it those last few times I had been there. Somehow I had to work through this for myself, find a way to stay sober and be happy. That's all, Jean, stay sober and be happy.

After pouring all the liquor down the sink, I went to the second floor, put on my pajamas, and crawled into bed. Florence had sent me some new publications from the Unity movement and I wanted to read them. These days I read almost anything my hands came upon. The answer was surely somewhere. Over the rainbow?

Unity is a religious group that thinks about God in ways entirely different from the way I ever had. The overruling concept was that God was in me. Funny, just like Emerson.

I read avidly and time moved quickly. I was not even aware of its passing. Nice.

When I did come to the end of the small book I was reading, my thoughts were racing. Unity spoke about growing, preparing oneself to the greatest degree of fulfillment. Spiritual growth.

Spiritual growth! But that's it, that's the answer, that's what it's all about! To grow spiritually and to understand self and then others. Mainly to envision life as a spiritual adventure, as an opportunity to learn awareness of Nature (God) and all things natural. The scheme of it all. I began to think about Toynbee and his views of those civilizations that survived because of the spiritual core. Here was value, the only kind that meant anything. It provided life with quality rather than the quantity of possession we all seemed to strive for.

I was excited, I felt alive. All the time I was reading, a quiet comfort and happiness overcame me. I had always hated the phrase "being at peace" but, undeniably, I was. But I was also filled with enthusiasm and eager to be on the road to spiritual growth.

Dawn was filtering through my bedroom window. It was early November and the colors were brilliant magenta. Thrilling. Dazzling and thrilling. The birth of a new day, a day for me to have for experience and growth.

Unity taught the expectation of happiness. No, they taught the expectation of all good things coming from one's inner feeling of happiness.

I felt happy. Elated. Oh, it was good to be alive, to be able to do. But what?

Old worry crept over me and I was again miserable. Suddenly I realized something I had been thinking about. I changed my entire outlook by changing my thoughts. While thinking happily and about expectations, I was exuberant. The moment I permitted my thoughts to be negative and brooding, I felt angry and frustrated, filled with uneasiness and disquiet.

That's a big secret, Jean. Thoughts *you* make dictate a mental and physical state.

I practiced. I began to think beautiful thoughts about the ocean and walking along the edge of the water. I thought about the dawn I'd just witnessed and I thought about being at work in a job I loved, whatever it might be.

And the thoughts again produced a sense of serenity and peace. I thought about God *in* me and I felt strangely comforted and happy.

I had stumbled upon a great truth, one that must have been hanging around for ages. Why hadn't I found it before? Maybe I wasn't ready for it.

But now I surely was.

I began to plan a new life. First I knew I had to move home with Mother, as much as I dreaded it. Oh, no . . . no negative thoughts. I forced myself to see it as an opportunity to grow. Brother, that's a real trick.

Anyway, I'd move home, sell my furniture, and rent my house. I couldn't bear to think about selling it. Renting would be difficult. But I knew I could do it, because I was beginning to see that my life had been filled with possessions that possessed me. How often had I said that I wish a time would come when everything I owned would be working at the same time . . . the vacuum cleaner, the refrigerator, and the thousand and one other appliances and mechanical gadgets I owned?

Now I wanted to strip myself down to me, to be rid of all possessions except the shell of the house. It was a bit scary. Everything gone? But I was determined to really make a new life, no halfway stuff.

I arose. This was the day for the beginning of an absolutely new life. I'd place an advertisement about my furniture and I'd see a realtor about renting the house. And today I'd begin dismantling it. While doing that, I'd think about what to do for income.

Purpose . . . that's what I'd needed. Now my purpose was clear. Start with the road to growing spiritually, rid self of possessions, and know that God is close by, *in* me. Still a strange thought. But I knew that I could grow with it. Lately God was truly out to lunch in Argentina for me. Now I wanted to feel the real presence.

Today. All of today, a beautiful day. I filled the house with music and was impatient for the newspaper office to open to place the classified advertisement for the furniture.

I began to go through my desk and throw things away. I had a tendency to keep things but I forced myself to really clean house. Everything. Remember, possessions possess.

I had turned the radio dial to the classical music station and Rachmaninoff was blaring throughout the house. My emotions soared with the music. How far I had come from one of my basic loves! My life seemed only to have been occupied with getting a drink, drinking, and recovering from drinking. Nothing else. But how did it all happen and for so long? I am an intelligent and professional woman, but all those years slipped by, all in an alcoholic daze. Years, decades, several decades!

The insidiousness of . . . alcoholism. Yes, say it. Get used to it. You were victimized by the disease of alcoholism and your life was nearly ruined. Amen.

Alcoholic. I hated the word. It reminded me of the three years in AA and having to say "My name is Jean and I'm an alcoholic." It was all true enough but I still hated it. It made me feel creepy, like a reject, like a victim of an unmentionable. The "disease of alcoholism" didn't sound nearly as bad. Anyway, I have a drinking problem, no matter what it's called, but I knew I wouldn't go back to AA. I knew I couldn't keep saying "I'm an alcoholic." Of course, if I didn't go back to AA, I'd certainly have to come to some way of understanding myself and my problem.

Weeks had passed and I was not drunk but I could feel the time bomb in me. Certainly that part would have to be changed. It had become noticeable to me that the longer the time stretched between, the more I wanted to be sober. I liked being without a headache, I liked knowing where I was all the time, I liked feeling good. However, there was still depression and the obsession with the thought of drinking and escape.

Depression would be a big problem to overcome. It began to

seem that the more candy I ate, the worse my depression became. My reading seemed to show this to be true, that many alcoholics are hypoglycemics. Trapped . . . no drinking, no candy, no ice cream, no depression.

Hold up, Jean. Stop getting into this bind. Accept this day, grow and be happy, practice being placid. Depression must stay in that period of hospitalization and psychiatry. Those dark, tunnel days of despairing . . . all for a small fee of $50,000. Hmmmmmmmmm. You're a real expensive hunk of flesh. Colleges, those graduated from and thrown out of, roughly maybe $50,000. And booze, for all those twenty-seven years, must surely have run another $50,000. And what about the hospitals? All the operations and long stays?

A real juicy piece of property, that's what you are. Now take care of the investment.

Looking at the clock, I saw it was time for me to get into action, to put my life into gear. I began to think about drinking, because I always drank when I was anticipating excitement, when I was excited about doing something, like a holiday feeling, the anticipation of something wonderful about to happen that never did. My body was not craving a drink, only my mind. So far it seemed to me that the mental craving was the worst to overcome. I was permitting my mind to drive me bananas with the obsession of wanting a drink, of wanting to drink. Obviously it was a habit I had formed and one that was deeply ingrained and would take much overcoming. There was also the element of being afraid of doing something . . . anything . . . without the aid of a drink, the crutch. What did I fear? People? Did I think I'd act foolishly?

Enough thinking. Time to act without a drink. See how it goes. I called the newspaper and placed an ad for the sale of the furniture, giving tomorrow evening as the first time it was available. I noticed my hands were wet with perspiration as I replaced the phone in its cradle. Ridiculous. Just ridiculous.

Dressing, I again found my thoughts on drinking. There had to be a way to get away from this. I suppose it has to do with replacement. Obviously I couldn't have been so occupied with drinking all those years without it possessing me. But would it take twenty-seven years to get rid of that mental habit? I had to keep busy and keep myself involved in more things than I could possibly do. Then worry about getting everything accomplished would replace thoughts of drinking. It would be a long process but it was the only way. That much I knew.

The first day the advertisement appeared, I had dozens of phone calls. By evening, when the people started to come to see my furniture, there was an almost frivolous atmosphere. I felt giddy, like it wasn't really happening, that the house being dismantled was not my own. I was thankful for these mental tricks.

John and Judy came. "You're not selling this desk? Or that dresser that you worked so hard to refinish?" John asked with incredulity.

"There's no place to put them over at my mother's home."

He looked at me searchingly and I felt a lump in my throat.

"Look. You and Judy take the chest of drawers and the bureau and I'll feel that they aren't gone. O.K.?"

"Of course we'll do that, if that's what you want."

"Yes. It is."

I also felt better about everything after that. Not everything was gone. When Sylvia heard that I was selling the furniture, she called from Florida and insisted that I keep almost everything for her. She was going to store it in a furniture warehouse for the time being.

The getting rid of furniture ended up with my selling several beds, kitchen furniture, radios, rugs, refrigerator, a washing machine—while all the pieces I cherished went to persons I loved. It had not been the disaster I first thought it would be.

The move to my mother's home was accomplished quickly. I moved into a small bedroom and tried to resign myself to knowing life would get better with effort on my part.

A young couple with two children moved into the farm, my only solution for keeping it.

Chapter 9

My father's death in 1971 seemed to underline my failure as a person. Until that time the part of me that showed to the world was an overachieving, seemingly successful woman, yet I knew the totality of my failures. The weeks, months, and years that followed were filled with trial and error and, on the surface, I seemed to be accomplishing nothing, for there were no honors, no awards, no titles of achievement. Just a plodding through a heavy sobriety that became lighter as I worked through ideas and concepts, keeping those that worked for me and discarding those that didn't.

There were failures in my attempt at an income, since I was unable to get a job because of my age. My try with an IBM composing business failed with many printers going out of business. I gave mail order a try, but that also failed. There was a period when I spent much time learning the relation of nutrition to alcoholism. My interest led me to the relation of pollution to cancer and the relation of processed food to cancer. I read Rachel Carson avidly, followed by a lot of reading about the population explosion.

My life was very empty except for working with changing my personality. Living with my mother reduced my living expenses to nothing and I managed a small income from the farm, but it wasn't enough to do anything. Taxes were paid and upkeep was maintained minimally.

Daily I put into practice everything I had learned and was learning about myself. Every morning I meditated before dawn. Then I watched dawn and put my life into thought reality. This was my growing time and, in it, I came to realize that life is meant only to prepare us for some greater journey, that when we die all we take with us is what we become while we are here.

During the infancy of the morning I was able to feel myself a part of the Universal Spirit.

But I was very lonely. There was a deep hole somewhere inside of me that I didn't know how to fill. No longer was I tantalized with thoughts of drinking, but my life was simply not what I wanted it to be. I had become deeply convinced that our lives reflect our thoughts and we mold and shape our lives from our thoughts. But I simply couldn't form the thought, because I didn't know what was missing or what I wanted to do. Could do. My professionalism was being wasted. There was much I knew academically but I couldn't seem to translate it into anything. I began to get back into my field of sociology, catching up on the reading I had missed. It was exciting.

But the core of loneliness stayed with me. There were many weekends when I drove to the parking lot of a shopping center and simply watched people. Very few were alone. Opportunities of living with another had presented themselves, but none was right. I knew it and was not about to get embroiled in something I couldn't undo. I was, and am, a person who needs to live alone to produce anything. In an involvement, my mind becomes too occupied with the trivia of daily living. There is no mental space. Yet, as I watched others, I envied them their cohabitation.

Then one night, during the evening news, I heard Walter Cronkite announce a segment about an old gentleman . . . eighty-one years old . . . who was taken by our government to South America or someplace to show them how to make bricks. The gentleman couldn't read or write but he made the best bricks in the world! That struck me hard; because he stayed at doing one thing and did it well, he was the world's expert in that. I, on the other hand, had tried my hand at a hundred things and never mastered any, simply because everything came too easily to me. What was I an expert in? Drinking! Just drinking.

That night I couldn't sleep because of thinking of that old man. Again I felt disgust with myself because all I knew was twenty-seven years of drinking. It was the only thing in my life that I stuck with through thick and thin.

So, Jean, you're an expert in drinking. Now you don't even do that anymore. You've just probably recovered, not having had a drink in four or five years, depending upon when you count from. How to recover without AA. That's what you're an expert in.

Suddenly it struck me. *That* was it! I did know one big ton of something about something. Drinking! Why hadn't I thought of it? Years ago, the first time in AA, I was in touch with Marty Mann and wanted to work with her then. Now, all these years later, it came through loud and clear. And what about all the time spent working with others?

I didn't sleep for the rest of the night. I began to plan to go to some alcoholism seminars and then I would write articles about alcoholism. That was very clear to me. My road was marked. *Clearly* marked. And I would begin to work with women alcoholics, those for whom AA didn't work.

When the dawn came, I had difficulty in knowing peace and calm, for I was very excited about my life. I knew that my future was charted just as clearly as I knew my name. I had something to say. I had gotten sober and stayed sober without craving or having to go to weekly meetings. I knew I had grown immeasurably, for my mental approach to life was changed. Everything about me was changed, and those who saw me also observed it. The change was real, not a temporary fluke. But it came from a conscious practice of what I knew I wanted . . . sobriety, happiness, emotional and spiritual growth, and purpose. Until this very minute, my new life had provided me with everything except purpose. Now I had a real purpose.

But where to begin? I knew that I had to formalize every

part of the process that changed me, to put into words the
things I now lived by.

THE PROGRAM

The Women for Sobriety program consists of Thirteen Statements of Acceptance. These are used daily to change our alcoholic negativism to positivism. Without doing this, sobriety is
ever a continuing battle, one that makes life a daily struggle.

It is suggested that the statements be read the first thing
each morning. Better still, time should be set aside each morning as a period for meditation upon the character of your life:
Do you know where you are going? Do you feel comfortable
about yourself? How will you enjoy today? What did you do
yesterday that was worthwhile? What are the reasons you want
to run away? What needs changing in your life?

Let us just suppose that you have made the decision to stop
drinking and want to begin a new life using the positive approach of the Women for Sobriety program. This begins with a
decision to accept responsibility for your life and for your actions. It means that your life of *reacting* to every situation is at
an end and that you have decided to change yourself into a person you can like and admire. This is the beginning.

You must buy a large loose-leaf notebook and, on
the first page, write: "This is the drinking history of

_____ (your name) _____ This may sound sophomoric but
it will serve an extremely useful purpose. Very often these
things that appear to be so simple turn out to be the most
helpful.

Our first statement is "I have a drinking problem that once
had me."

Every one of us has a drinking problem, some of us more
than others. When we are drinking, this problem truly *has* us,
because our life is dictated by the liquor we need to have in
order to live.

We are forced to change liquor stores; we must find hiding

places for bottles; we must think up hundreds of little lies to cover our actions; we must appear sober and calm and in control when actually we are falling apart physically, mentally, and emotionally; we must try to explain away the money we've spent for liquor; we are finally forced to vodka so as not to give off so many fumes; we must keep our hands from shaking; we must . . .

On and on it goes. Yes, we are in the grip of alcohol. It *has* us. We have no free will once we've started drinking.

How many times did I ask myself what I found so thrilling about drinking when it only brought unhappiness, loneliness, sickness, depression? I wasn't "living," I was only breathing to feed an addiction. Is this what you are doing with your life?

To change requires a decision, a conscious decision to end all the misery you endure and that which you create for others. It is the beginning of accepting the responsibility for yourself and your actions. Just "thinking" about it won't work.

Alcoholic women have much greater trouble with overcoming their problem than men, and my opinion is that women have difficulty with making an absolute decision. They *think* about quitting someday. They *want* to quit. Or they say "I wonder if I'm strong enough to quit?" or "I wonder if I *really* can?"

Don't question, KNOW! Make a STATEMENT and then hang on to that statement with dear life. Treat it like your security blanket, for that is precisely what it is. It takes an absolute decision to give up self-disgust and replace it with changing yourself. It requires a decision to manage your life rather than be managed by liquor.

These are strong words. They are meant to be. Women are notoriously wishy-washy because so many generations have programed them to feel that way.

But you can change that. You are a thinking, capable woman.

In your notebook, draw a line down the center of the page, making it into two columns. Above the left side on the top line write "Times I have been happy when drinking in the past three years." And on the top line of the other half of the page write "Times I have been unhappy when drinking in the past three years." Be sure to include the times you have been sick.

On this first day of your new life, keep yourself *very busy*. The object is *to try* to overcome the obsessive thoughts about drinking that will plague you. You are walking around with a time bomb inside you that spells DISASTER. This time bomb cannot go off if you defuse it and that is done by not drinking.

On this first day, use will power and don't drink. Prove to yourself that you have strength of character that you weren't sure of or even thought you didn't have.

You are responsible for your actions today and every day. You may be an otherwise brilliant businesswoman with the exception of your attitude and actions in regard to your drinking. In this area you need help, need to be led at first, need to be shown how to do it.

We are all alcoholics together; we need help from each other. We need encouragement. We need understanding.

This day, this first day, feel good about your decision and never weaken. Stick to what you know you want to do.

Our second statement is "Negative emotions destroy only myself."

This is the second day into the journey of learning about yourself as a woman. As drinking women, we know that negative emotions destroy us. As alcoholics we are filled with fears that are negativisms of life, of living.

Emerson wrote, "We are afraid of truth, afraid of death, afraid of each other." From these inherent fears, we become negative, sullen, withdrawn, unable to cope. We drink to overcome but our fears only become worse. We then become resentful.

When we think ill of another, do we hurt them? If we simmer with unexpressed ill feelings, who do we hurt? Is anything achieved with bitterness?

Negative emotions cripple the spirit and paralyze thinking. Very often these negative emotions come from our feelings of inadequacy. We often think badly of others because we think badly of ourselves.

It would appear logical that we can overcome the negativism only as soon as we are able to make ourselves into someone we might admire. Our overcoming is in exact proportion to our becoming someone worthwhile.

Negative emotions not only destroy us in subtle ways but they keep anything good from happening to us. A negative woman attracts only negative responses from others.

Who is affected by our negative emotions? Do we achieve anything with bitterness? Are we able to function as an adult? Do our resentments make life easier to tolerate?

In your diary of self, (a) make a long list of as many resentments as you can think of. Write down every negative thought, remembrance, idea that your mind permits you to recall.

(b) Next to each one, write what you think to be the reason for it and how it started. (c) Write the result of your bitterness or resentment. Did it make the situation better, more tolerable, happier?

For your third day of the journey into sobriety and into learning about yourself, spend the day learning the third statement of acceptance. Memorize it so that it will be in your mind to act upon. "Happiness is a habit I will develop."

Notice that this acceptance says "will develop." I am making the assumption, based upon my own experience, that you have not developed the habit of happiness, although I may be wrong. However, very few women alcoholics that I know, or have known, are happy.

For many years I was convinced that some people are just naturally happy and others are not. Most of the time, I was not happy. I seemed to be waiting for the time when everything would change and be perfect. Then I'd be happy.

But how do we learn happiness? It begins with the realization of our whole person, of finding out what we really are, what we can become, what we really think.

All this, however, is conditioned. We are a composite of the residue of our responses to conditions, past and present. We respond to situations according to the mental environment in which we live. If we are angry, our response to anything will be negative. If we are uncaring, we will have little or no response to anything. If we are guilt-ridden, our response will reflect this.

Therefore, we must condition ourselves for happiness so that we can elicit only beneficial responses. Certainly no one would ever say "Well, I think I should develop a habit of feeling guilty" or any other such ill feelings.

But it is valid to say "I will develop a habit for happiness." To do this, we must improve our mental environment. We must think happiness and it will follow.

Most of us know that Abraham Lincoln once said that people are just about as happy as they permit themselves to be. So much of the time we do not permit ourselves pleasant emotions because we seem to be too busy with negative emotions such as guilt, remorse, despair, or ennui.

In your diary of self, (a) make a list of all the times you have been *very happy*. (b) Now make a list of what you think would make you happy this very minute.

(c) At the end of this third day, after having practiced being happy all day, make an entry about how your day was.

"Problems bother me only to the degree I permit them to." This is your fourth day into the experience of self.

Have you ever heard anyone say "Well, that just gives me something else to worry about"?

I suppose I'm not telling you anything new when I say that women alcoholics are great worriers. I was, and very probably you are.

Worry never changed anything except to make us drink more, hoping that whatever we are worrying about will go away. Worry is the drinking woman's first enemy. Worry about not being caught, worry about how to manage drinking, worry about how to get more liquor, worry about the children finding out, worry about the family's finances, worry about the job, worry, worry, worry.

Of course, worry is not such a great friend to the sober woman either.

Worry undermines every real chance to succeed at being and staying sober. How often have I read that the things we worry about happen less than 1 per cent of the time?

Try thinking about the things you worried about and see if they happened the way you were afraid they would.

In your diary of self, (a) write several paragraphs about specific problems that once worried you. (b) Next, list how these problems were eventually solved and make a note about whether or not they were solved the way you worried about them.

Answer the following questions: Do your problems keep you awake at night? Do your problems make you drink? (Or did they?) Do your worries keep you from enjoying life? Do your problems bother you to the degree that they disrupt your life?

Write a long paragraph in your diary entitled "How my worrying solved my problems."

Make a definite list of recent worries. To the right side of each item, write how it turned out.

Our fifth Statement of Acceptance is "I am what I think." Foolish? If you practice this for six months, I'll bet you won't be laughing anymore.

But it requires practice. It took me a very long time to manage this statement but I began to use early morning meditation time to manage it.

Our drinking reinforced our self-destructive behavior and thoughts. Our behavior from drinking makes us want to destroy the woman we are because we cannot stand her actions. Here again is the merry-go-round. We don't like what we are, so we drink. Then we hate even more the person the drinking produces. So we drink more to forget. And over and over and over.

It is easy to see that part of our drinking comes from the dislike of self and this later becomes disgust with self. Part of the solution to overcoming our drinking problem is to change our feelings about ourselves and this change must begin with changing the image of ourselves.

What has changing the image got to do with drinking? The philosophy behind the whole program of Women for Sobriety is based upon the concept of our thoughts creating the world in which we live. First the thought and then the action. Our actions carry out our thoughts so, to have a happy life, we must have, *first*, happy thoughts. To be a person whom we admire rather than for whom we feel disgust, we must, *first*, form a positive mental image.

This is difficult for alcoholic women especially, for we are so accustomed to thinking negatively about ourselves. Now we must begin with forming a likable, lovable woman in our minds.

Begin saying to yourself "I am a capable, competent woman who is filled with strength and confidence."

We must begin forming our world by beginning with our mental environment and accepting responsibility for our thoughts . . . which dictate the actions to follow. No longer can we allow, or permit, circumstances to mold us. We are larger than circumstances.

We are the architects of our thoughts and these are the producers of actions. We are the mistresses of what we are and what we become. We dictate events from this moment forward.

Exercise your mind and direct your thoughts. The effects will demonstrate to you that your thoughts are responsible for what happens to you.

In your diary, use single words to describe what you think about yourself. Use between thirty and fifty. For example: "kind," "stubborn," "loving," "destructive," "resentful," "angry," etc.

When you have finished that list, make another list, just as long, using the words to describe what you want to be, such as: "sober," "happy," "compassionate," etc.

The second list is to be read every morning and every night until doomsday.

Childish you say? Scoff at it *now*, but first try it. It works. During the day, recite your list to yourself, saying "I am a happy woman," etc. This is a form of self-hypnosis, I suppose, but you will notice that, as your mind adjusts to these programed thoughts, your actions will follow.

I can only say that, if you want a happy life, this is the way it can be had.

Our sixth statement is "Life can be ordinary or it can be

great." I suppose this is a simplistic truism but there are times when we must be reminded of it. It is not that we do not know it. I suppose all womankind and mankind would immediately agree to it, that life can either be ordinary or it can be great.

Again we get to our basic philosophy. Life cannot be great unless we begin to put something into it and that must come about through our thoughts. Life cannot be anything but dull if that is the way we think it will be.

But what helps us to make it great? What is it that puts some real zest into it? What changes it? Obviously we must change our attitude toward life and this begins with our making ourselves exude enthusiasm.

Enthusiasm is an attitude. There are some persons who can make buying a tomato an exciting experience, while others see this simply as something that has to be done.

The difference between these two is that one person sees it as a fun experience and brings enthusiasm to the chore while the other sees it as merely a chore.

Too often we are duped into believing that these feelings *come* to us. The truth of it is that we must first make these feelings. *Then* we *experience* them and the results produced by them.

To make life great has much to do with the quality of living we invest in life. Drinking removed quality from life. It removed us from life. Drinking cancels all possibility of enthusiasm but I always believed that it added zest to mine, rarely considering the bad moments that followed.

Have you ever known anyone who is always trying something new? Have you ever known anyone who is always excited about life?

For your diary entry this sixth day, write about everything new you have tried in the last six months. Have you done anything that really excited you? Have you walked, or jogged, or just enjoyed a sunset? Have you had new ideas? Have you seen or heard anything that inspired you? Have you met anyone interesting? Have you had any ideas about making your life count?

Now, do something entirely new today, something you have

never done before. It makes absolutely no difference what it is so long as it is something you have never before done.

After you have done something new, write about it *in detail* in your diary. If it was inspiring, write about it. If it was just fun, write about it. But whatever you did, write about it in detail and tell how you liked doing it.

And now to the seventh day, the seventh statement. Again, a truism, but one we must act upon to make it into reality: "Love can change the course of my world."

Who doesn't agree with this? If we are able to be overcome, to permit ourselves to feel feelings of love, other emotions of a negative nature will automatically be removed because love replaces them.

Great idea, but it's the doing that presents the problem. All of us are willing, but are we able to overcome with love?

Love is oftentimes difficult for the woman who knew a drinking problem. Too often she sealed herself away from others because, when drinking, she was forced to remove herself bodily and emotionally.

When drinking, the art of loving is sometimes a stranger. It is said that we learn to love by loving. Sort of a learn by doing, an on-the-job training.

To love is to grow, for it is an emotion that takes us outside ourselves. When we love we put aside our total concern for self-interests; our thoughts are other than self, they are turned outward.

Loving others is not the easiest assignment, yet its rewards are very great, great enough so that we should work at love every day. Eric Hoffer says, "It is easier to love humanity as a whole than to love one's neighbor." But we must begin with loving each other in a real feeling of oneness. We should never distrust each other, for we have a common bond as women and, most especially, as women bonded together by the same illness.

Is love a degree of awareness of each other? Is it involvement with trust? Is love caring enough to come together to share bad and good experiences? Is love compassion and empathy for another woman's problem?

Love is all of these. Love also involves other than people; it can involve the natural world and the beauty in it. Ethel Barrymore once said, "You must learn day by day, year by year, to broaden your horizon. The more things you love, the more you are interested in, the more you enjoy, the more you are indignant about—the more you have left when anything happens." Love insulates us against the chill of self-doubt.

In your diary, (a) make a list of the people you love and try to identify the reason (or reasons) you love them. (b) Then make a list of the persons you have difficulty loving and try to give the reason. Following this, write a paragraph or two about what you think love is and how it changes your world.

Our eighth statement is "The fundamental object of life is emotional and spiritual growth." Perhaps this should be two Statements of Acceptance but it is my belief that with emotional growth comes spiritual growth. In any case, we must ever try to grow in mind and heart.

All things are in a constant state of change. To see the change as a form of growth is, in itself, growth. Emotional growth comes from frequent introspection with an eye toward changing for the better. Emotional growth is the extraction of something useful from traumatic situations.

Continued emotional growth prevents unhappiness. It provides us a course of life to be pursued. When emotional growth is coupled with spiritual growth, the mind and soul are filled with a sense of well-being.

Can there possibly be anything more important in life than emotional and spiritual growth? How often do we permit ourselves to remember that all we take with us when we leave this earth is what we become when we are on it? Growth is more than simply something to do to fill time. It is our reason for being, for existing. It is the essence of life.

Spiritual growth is something more than getting over temper tantrums or resentments or pettiness. It is much deeper and far more complicated to achieve. Do we really "achieve" it? I think not. It is more felt, more assimilated, more experienced than anything.

Spiritual growth is a very individual matter. What I might

consider spiritual growth might not be to someone else. It is, however, a sense of peace within one's own spirit, one's soul.

I feel spiritual in the observation of Nature, for then my spirit floats free and joins in an otherworldly force. I feel a oneness with the universe when seeing dawn and sunrise, two distinctly different events. An eighteenth-century metaphysical poet suggested we see the universe in a grain of sand. Each particle is representative of the whole. All of us are part of the sum and, all being a part of the total, are responsible for ourselves and for others.

Emerson wrote, "To speak truly, few adult persons can see nature. . . . The lover of nature is he [she] whose inward and outward senses are still truly adjusted to each other . . . whose intercourse with heaven and earth becomes part of his [her] daily food."

While watching the dawn and the sunrise, permit your spirit to soar above the ordinary. (So much of our life must be concerned with it so much of the time.) Experience the sounds of the silence that envelops you. Know a spiritual oneness with the universe.

In your diary, write, in detail, your feelings about the dawn and the sunrise. Describe every feeling you experienced. Explain what you believe emotional and spiritual growth to be.

The ninth statement of our program is "The past is gone forever." For me, I can only say "Hurrah!" In this program we forget the past, plan for tomorrow, and live today.

I have been criticized for this position but I do not see any value to be had from a constant reiteration of past misdeeds and misconduct. I do not have to talk about my past continually to know it is there. My biggest task in life is to work at forgetting it.

Life is centered in the NOW, in the present moment. How often do we hear it said that all we have is the present moment? It is frequently said because it is true.

Of course we have the past if we perpetuate it in our memories and if we drag it along with us into every other moment we live. We must liberate ourselves from *what was* in order to be free for *what is*. *What is* and how we act sets the stage for what will then be *what was*.

The message is to forget the past. It is over and done; it cannot come back. We are fools to continue to react to it. The real issue is how we handle ourselves in the present so that we do not make the same ugly and upsetting mistakes. That is advice for myself. Does it pertain to you?

When I was drinking I was forever looking forward to something in the future, or I was reciting something from the past. I was never in the present. Only recently have I come to grasp that every day is a tomorrow and will be a yesterday.

People who live in the past must give way to those who move toward the future. How often have we seen this in elderly persons, their preoccupation with the past and its annoyance to those younger, who are centered in events to come and not those gone?

For most alcoholics, thinking about the past awakens regret and this is an emotion we can ill afford. There will be times when we must extract something from our past and make use of it but we cannot dwell on it nor can we constantly relive or retell it. Our only interest in the past is for it to act as a guide, a map, for the future. If we have a past that was directionless, then it must tell us to act differently so that we have a future with a direction.

We cannot afford to live in the past, for it will bankrupt us. Life is for living and not for recalling.

A great part of being centered in the NOW is to keep oneself busy. Boredom invites recollection and remorse. Fill each day to the brim. Become involved in activities that serve a purpose. We must always savor moments but not overfill them lest we again try to escape from ourselves.

In your diary, (a) write your plans for the remaining part of the day. (b) Now write your plans for the week, and (c) write your plans for the month. On a separate page (d) write your plans for the year: what you want to do, where you want to go, who you wish to see, and what you want to accomplish.

The tenth statement is "All love given returns twofold." There is not much that is very mysterious about this statement.

It is very much like the seventh statement but worded more emphatically. It would seem that the degree to which we can forget self, in whatever we do, is the degree to which we will enjoy emotional return.

All of this is true enough, but for alcoholic women like ourselves, this statement becomes very difficult when applied. In theory we readily agree. Giving and receiving love for alcoholic women is a real taskmaster, because love is a precious commodity that few of us know how to accept or cherish or give. For us, sometimes the "giving" of love is far easier than accepting it. We want love . . . yearn for it . . . but we are often unable to accept it because of not trusting it, fearing that it will suddenly be withdrawn or that the expression of it is not valid or true because we feel unworthy of love.

Learning to put this statement into action is one of the more difficult ones. It involves trust and a belief in ourselves. We must begin to exercise what we have been trying to learn: that we are capable, competent, and able to give love freely, with our whole hearts. Moreover, that we will accept love returned to us. We will accept it in the spirit that we are worthy of it.

And why not? We are women reaching out to others by way of our new self-awareness, which tells us that we are perfectly capable of giving love to others and are able to receive their returned love and concern and caring for us.

As an exercise in recovery and as a continuing exercise in living, do something very special for someone by making a forceful effort. Visit someone who is lonely, give encouragement to someone who seems depressed, take someone to lunch who is never able to go. And after doing one of these things, savor the happiness you created for that other person. Feel happy with yourself. Determine that this will become a habit.

In your diary, write about the emotions you experienced before and after. Write about each nuance of feeling you knew. Describe the interchange of emotions, what you gave and what you received.

This is your eleventh day into sobriety and you should now be feeling very good. Naturally, you will be feeling good enough so that you will think you no longer have a drinking problem. But you do. Read back over your diary for the first three days and remember clearly how you then felt. You do have a drinking problem that is a disease. To treat this disease and be happy requires new patterns of thought as a way to happiness.

Our eleventh statement is "Enthusiasm is my daily exercise." Enthusiasm is as infectious as a new viral strain. Let one woman have it and everyone in the room is affected. Of course this is also true of someone who is depressed. Others feel the negativism and react to it. From this we should conclude that each of us can affect others by what we exude.

Probably one of the greatest errors in my thinking over most of the years of my life has to do with my faulty assumption that people are automatically happy or enthusiastic or confident. This is simply not true. We are not born that way. *We become that way through our own efforts.*

Enthusiasm doesn't suddenly descend on us. It comes to us through practice. So, today, begin the practice of enthusiasm. Be vitally interested in everything today and *feel* enthusiastic about everything. Feel supercharged about the weather, no matter what it is. Exude interest and enthusiasm with whomever you come into contact. Feel like a package of energy looking for a place to express itself. Make your thoughts think about life with enthusiasm.

And, today, even if you must force yourself every minute, give off enthusiasm. Today is the beginning of this constant exercise of personality. Enthusiasm requires learning, concentration, and practice.

In your diary, (a) list the earlier times in your life when you remember feeling enthusiastic. (b) Describe the reaction of others to your display of enthusiasm today. (c) Did you like the way you felt today? Describe it in detail.

On this, the twelfth day of your journey into sobriety and learning about yourself, practice the twelfth statement: "I am a competent woman and have much to give others." This is true, you know. Well, probably you *don't* know it, but take it from me, it is quite true. Each of us is uniquely different and each of us is capable of something that no one else is capable of.

Alcoholic women are intelligent and hypersensitive. Emotionally, they are easily hurt, too overly generous, too conscientious, too easily overcome with guilt and depression. All these emotions tend to cloud over any sense of belief in self. The negative emotions tend to make us have little regard for ourselves; we feel unimportant, unneeded, and unworthy.

Perhaps society's attitude toward the alcoholic woman has had some part in giving us this feeling. Perhaps not. Perhaps we have created this image all by ourselves with the aid of alcohol. Maybe we were that way and alcohol made it worse.

In any case, we are competent women when we permit ourselves to be. We are capable of great accomplishment, but we can only reach this fullness with complete belief in ourselves and our capabilities. This is our true liberation, the freeing ourselves of all that baggage of despair and self-pity and guilt and depression.

Make a diary entry of all that you are capable of doing, such as: repair appliances, be a loyal friend, play the piano or sing, do bookkeeping, fly a plane, teach children, draw or sketch, direct plays or groups or lead meetings, speak a foreign language, drive a car, make out income tax returns, etc. Be sure to include everything. Each of us is uniquely different from all others. It is up to us to find our skills, our competency.

Make a diary entry of all your accomplishments and make a second list of all that you are going to do. Be assertive in your ideas and plans.

And the last of our acceptance statements is the one that should be the most important to you as time moves onward and upward. It reads "I am responsible for myself and my sisters."

We are all responsible for ourselves, for our actions and reactions, for our effect on others, for our attitudes and being. We make ourselves and our actions. We must then accept the responsibility of what we have created (or destroyed).

With the acceptance of this program and with the application of yourself to its principles, you will be on a program of mind development which will create new habits. From these you will learn to know confidence in yourself; you will gain new strengths.

Grab hold of this program. Understand yourself as a woman who is capable and who must no longer mistreat or punish herself. Ask yourself *why* you punished yourself all those years. Make a final diary entry about why you think you punished yourself for so long a time.

Learning what you have learned about yourself, prepare now to lead other women into learning about themselves. Help them to find the way out of the darkness of alcoholism. This each of us is responsible for doing and accomplishing.

Emotional growth is happiness; spiritual growth is peace. Together these create a competent, loving woman.

Chapter 10

Women everywhere confirmed my opinion that women alcoholics needed something additional to Alcoholics Anonymous or something alternative to it. Women alcoholics needed something more, something special, because alcoholic women feel that they have failed . . . as wives, as mothers, as daughters, as women. Women carry great burdens of guilt from the feeling of this failure which society . . . our culture . . . continually reinforces. Out of this guilt comes depression.

Alcoholics Anonymous has been the single most successful help available to alcoholics for forty years. There is no one that could challenge this. Alcoholics the world over have managed and controlled their alcoholism with the use of the AA program of twelve steps. Up to now, no other program has come along to offer any more or any different help. But despite its great successes, only 6 to 10 per cent of all alcoholics ever get to AA and only 3½ to 5 per cent of all women alcoholics ever do. There is a general belief that almost all alcoholics are getting help through Alcoholics Anonymous. Nothing could be further from the truth.

Women for Sobriety, like Alcoholics Anonymous, is loosely knit by self-help groups of women who meet as often as they choose to meet. Some groups meet several times a week and some groups meet only once a week.

Alcoholics Anonymous has a program of twelve steps, which its members "work"; that is, they use these steps upon which to model their lives. Women for Sobriety uses a method of Thirteen Statements of Acceptance upon which its members reshape their lives. A glance at the two programs will immediately present some of the differences:

AA

1. We admitted we were powerless over alcohol . . . that our lives had become unmanageable.

2. Came to believe that a Power greater than ourselves could restore us to sanity.

3. Made a decision to turn our will and our lives over to the care of God *as we understood Him.*

4. Made a searching and fearless moral inventory of ourselves.

5. Admitted to God, to ourselves, and to another human being the exact nature of our wrongs.

6. Were entirely ready to have God remove all these defects of character.

7. Humbly asked Him to remove our shortcomings.

8. Made a list of all persons we had harmed and became willing to make amends to them all.

9. Made direct amends to such people wherever possible, except when to do so would injure them or others.

WFS

1. I have a drinking problem that once had me.

2. Negative emotions destroy only myself.

3. Happiness is a habit I will develop.

4. Problems bother me only to the degree I permit them to.

5. I am what I think.

6. Life can be ordinary or it can be great.

7. Love can change the course of my world.

8. The fundamental object of life is emotional and spiritual growth.

9. The past is gone forever.

10. All love given returns twofold.

11. Enthusiasm is my daily exercise.

12. I am a competent woman and have much to give others.

13. I am responsible for myself and my sisters.

10. Continued to take personal inventory and when we were wrong promptly admitted it.

11. Sought through prayer and meditation to improve our conscious contact *with God as we understood Him,* praying only for knowledge of His will for us and the power to carry them out.

12. Having had a spiritual awakening as the result of these steps, we tried to carry this message to alcoholics, and to practice these principles in all our affairs.

The Women for Sobriety program is an affirmation of the value and worth of each woman. It is a program that leads each woman to asserting her belief in self, a program that leads her to seeing herself in a positive and self-confident image. She will see herself as forceful and compassionate, assertive and warm, capable and caring, resourceful and responsible.

The Women for Sobriety program centers on the woman as the AA program cannot do, because it was not intended to. Historically, the AA program came into being when it was still believed that very few women had a drinking problem! Today we know that there are as many women alcoholics as men and, as women assume more responsible positions in this fast-paced society, their number is growing.

The earlier assumption that only a few women are alcoholics is mirrored in a society that continually lags in treatment for these many women. Out of six hundred halfway houses, only thirty are for women alcoholics. Treatment facilities of all types and kinds lag in providing adequate treatment for women. And whan women are released from treatment facilities, they *have* only AA or nothing and, for a variety of reasons, many choose nothing.

Many women's emotional problems and disturbances are all tied up in the male-female relationship; rehabilitation via a male-female organization is not the answer at that specific time. Many women utilize the Women for Sobriety all-woman setting and are then able, after a period of time and after finding some self-dignity, to go to AA.

All women in our culture feel a modicum of guilt for not being "perfect," for not fitting into the unrealistic mold that American society has cast for them. For alcoholic women, this guilt is almost unbearable at times. When the feelings about this guilt are shared with other women who also experience it, the guilt can be alleviated. It can become a thing of the past. Women alcoholics have this strong feeling of having failed as a wife, as a mother, as a sister or daughter, as a woman. Their alcoholism and recovery is all involved with the removal of these guilt feelings.

On the other hand, the male alcoholic feels much remorse for having hurt his family . . . his wife and his children. He rarely feels *guilt* and he never feels the same as women do. There is a vast and distinct difference in this particular area between male and female alcoholics.

And there are many other differences. As a result of these excessive guilt feelings, women cannot get their act together. They have great difficulty with feeling good about themselves, much less feeling confident and worthy. Remove the alcohol and these overwhelming feelings of guilt and failure set in and possess.

Studies show that women have a much greater struggle in recovering from alcoholism. It takes them a longer period of time and more therapy, *yet they have the least amount of help available.* However, when women do manage recovery, they stay recovered for longer periods of time. There is a lower rate of relapse than among men, perhaps because women remember how far they can slip back.

Outside an institution, the alcoholic woman is most often living within the environment that nurtures her problem, which can only be overcome when she (a) has a desire to overcome and (b) changes her mental environment, her habits, her thoughts, her actions and reactions, her life responses.

How she learns to view herself as capable of overcoming not only her drinking problems but other problems as well is a basic task of the Women for Sobriety program. This change of self and the perception of self is reinforced by the group, which is comprised of women each of whom is making an effort to learn positive responses to life's stress.

Alcoholic women's shortcomings are compensated for with the behavior of escapism, which frequently emerges in some form of addiction. In this case, alcohol addiction. The escape from reality is sought to avoid the reality of pain and stress and the inability and/or desire to cope.

Eventually, however, this form of escape, that once sufficed for all problems, itself produces pain, the pain of addiction. Again life's pattern is repeated. From childhood onward, those who become alcoholics have known more tensions, fewer satisfactions, and fewer ways of handling stress. Many had rejecting mothers and/or domineering mothers; most were brought up in families lacking in understanding or not displaying warmth or affection. Those most common personality traits of alcoholics—anger, depression, insecurity, restlessness, conflict, anxiety, low frustration tolerance, guilt, lack of self-esteem, emotional instability, and guilt—come from this familiar trauma. Poorly defined parental roles or the lack of one parent or the grave stress displayed between parents creates the alcoholic's psychological desire to flee from life.

Women for Sobriety groups provide acceptance and nurture, they provide kinship and identification; they provide supportive love, help, and care; they are nonjudgmental; they reinforce faltering self-esteem; they provide a place to be rid of anxiety; they provide friendship with others of the same mind and circumstances; they provide a place of trust; and they provide a forum for those women who need to talk and relate.

The entire program put forth by Women for Sobriety is an ongoing learning experience. The group only partially provides the way. The Thirteen Statements of Acceptance provide the means when used as suggested as a part of each day's commitment.

The thirteen statements that comprise the central core of the program provide a way of viewing and living life in a way that differs from earlier defensive behavioral response. It is a form of reality therapy that changes the alcoholic woman's negative defensiveness to positive action through a learning of self.

THIRTEEN STATEMENTS OF ACCEPTANCE

1. *"I Have a Drinking Problem That Once Had Me"*
Acknowledgment of our illness as a problem is the prime factor in our recovery . . . It is necessary for us to face the reality of our addiction but not be overwhelmed by it.

For a long time I struggled with the acceptance of my drinking problem. I'm ashamed to say that, to the very bitter end, I still thought that I might possibly manage it. Only the continual illness and the collapse of my body made me acknowledge and accept my problem as an actual fact. I knew that I had lost all control. Actually, I had lost control more than ten years earlier.

How can a normally intelligent woman refuse to admit that she has a drinking problem?

This is the key to alcoholism; overcoming denial is the start of recovery. We want to keep the problem more than we want to be rid of it. We want to keep it because we can't imagine living without alcohol. Denial is the biggest obstacle before recovery can happen. We deny we have a drinking problem because we use the alcohol for need fulfillment.

Our rehabilitation begins with our acceptance of having a drinking problem but that it will no longer have us. That with our acknowledgment of our inordinate dependence upon alcohol, we can put ourselves to the task of finding out why we became so dependent. We must discover why we turned to alcohol in times of trouble. My experience shows that I used alcohol to fill emotional needs. I used alcohol to avoid problems. I used alcohol to produce a personality that I liked better than the one I had without alcohol. I used alcohol to run away from myself and from the person I considered to be worthless and unlovable . . . me. My constant running away helped me to deny my problem. Denial became my biggest problem.

I have a drinking problem but it no longer has me. It no longer controls me. I am the master of it and I am the master of myself.

Why did I need to run? Am I still running from myself?

Do you know your emotional needs and how to meet them? Do you recognize the emotional situations that once led you to drinking but now you control in other ways?

For those who are still drinking, examine the circumstances you are involved in just before you begin drinking. See if you can find the emotion that leads you to that first drink.

Your illness of alcoholism will always be in your life but you need never be ill again, for as you accept your problem, you are already beginning to control it and your life.

2. *"Negative Emotions Destroy Only Myself"*
As drinking women, we know that negative emotions are disastrous. We have probably been ruled by them for long periods of time, periods during which our negativism took the form of defensiveness and fears.

We are sometimes sullen, withdrawn, unable to cope. There are times we drink to overcome but we only intensify our fears and our negativisms.

Our negative emotions often come from thinking ill of another, from feelings of resentments. When we think badly of another, is that person hurt? No; we are the ones that feel it. If we simmer with unexpressed ill feelings, whom do we hurt? Is anything achieved with our negative emotion?

Negative emotions cripple the spirit and paralyze thinking. Very often these negative emotions come from our feelings of inadequacy. We often think ill of ourselves, and from these feelings, we permit bitterness an open door.

I speak from experience, from a long lifetime of negative feelings that controlled me to the exclusion of everything else. These negative feelings were all born out of deep feelings of inadequacy, of feeling not capable of matching others.

I like the Chinese concept of non-competition, of not competing with each other but doing whatever it is just for the joy of doing it. This brings out the best in most of us. Usually it is the aspect of competition that is so threatening, each of us being measured against others.

Competition arouses feelings of inadequacy and this brings forth great feelings of negativism through anger, anguish and bad feelings toward others.

We often think badly of others because we think badly of ourselves. We can only overcome this when we are able to make ourselves into someone we can admire. Our overcoming is in exact proportion to our becoming.

Negative emotions destroy us in so many, many ways. So long as we have a single negative emotion, we will be kept from anything very positive happening to us. A negative woman attracts only negative responses from others.

The most important aspect of negative feelings is that these feelings always precede drinking bouts. A state of "what's the use," or "who cares?" is the initiator for escape from reality.

Overcoming these feelings of worthlessness is part of this acceptance. These feelings create the negativisms that destroy us.

3. *"Happiness Is a Habit I Will Develop"*
This statement may seem almost too Pollyanna-ish for today's woman, who is working hard to be herself, her real self; one who is working through her angers and resentments to find the core of those emotions. And happiness? Doesn't that come by itself, after everything else is understood and erased? When we are over our hang-ups?

I am all for the realization of our whole person, of finding out what we really are and then working through all of the negativisms to find cause. Behavior is conditioned. We are a residue of our responses to conditions, past and present. We respond to situations according to that which is in our mind, residing there to be acted upon.

If we are angry, our response to all things will be negative. If we are uncaring we will have little or no feeling toward anything.

Conditioning oneself to happiness can only elicit beneficial responses. There are many cynics who believe that to seek happiness, or even to consider happiness as something one develops, is naïve. But cynics are among those who are always unhappy, never permitting themselves to learn the secret.

For many years I was convinced that some people were just naturally happy and others were not. And most of the time, I was not happy. I was too deep into my feeling sorry for myself, waiting for the time when everything in my life would miraculously change and then instant happiness would follow.

Happiness never came to me until I learned the secret of making it for myself, of finding an inner glow that somehow made all other things right.

Happiness comes from our attitudes. We must create it for ourselves.

4. *"Problems Bother Me Only to the Degree I Permit Them To"*
This statement is one of the most effective in providing a change in life-style and it is probably the most effective for me. As you probably know, all of these statements are the method I used to find a new life. Learning that I didn't have to react to everything with upsetting emotions was an important part of my recovery.

Many times, when I am reacting to events, I realize that I am permitting myself to react because I am allowing whatever the trouble is to bother me.

The value of this statement is in learning that we can control our reactions, that we needn't react at all. We permit ourselves to be bothered by people, things, events, actions.

If we are upset, if we are depressed, if we are sad, if we are lonely, if we are angry, it is because we permit ourselves to feel these emotions. And to react to them.

Whatever it is that bothers you, it needn't. You do not have to react to it.

Worry comes under this category. Have you ever heard anyone say, "Well, that just gives me something else to worry about"?

Women with a drinking problem are great worriers. We seem to worry about all things, big and small. But worry never changed anything, except to make it all worse. I have often read that the thing we worry about happens about 1 per cent of the time.

Worry is an excellent example of letting ourselves react to a negative emotion. The problem we are worrying about can only bother us to the degree we permit it to. This is true of all negative emotions we permit.

5. "I Am What I Think"

Do you know your own mind? Do you know why you think it? Are you aware of the mental place in which you live, the real environment that you create for yourself by your thoughts? Or do you just let it happen?

Almost everything we experience is a result of our thought. With our mind, we shape our day.

Have you ever dropped several things and said, "Boy, this just isn't my day. Everything I touch, falls." And then, for the remainder of the day, that's exactly what continues to happen.

Your day was programmed from the start by the thought you gave yourself, "This isn't my day, everything goes wrong." You also made yourself unreceptive to good thoughts and creative actions. You brainwashed yourself negatively.

We are free to think whatever we choose to think. We can think happy thoughts or unhappy thoughts. When we are troubled or distressed, our mind has caused it. And our mind can erase these feelings. We know that it can heal us.

Even though we know these things about our mind, it is sometimes hard to mold our thinking, for we have been subjected to so many years of negative preconditionings. We are oftentimes victims rather than victors over mind.

Try an experiment to show the power of mental imaging. Think about a very gloomy day—pounding rain on a dull, gray day. You are late in leaving your apartment in getting off to work. Then the car doesn't start and you must call a mechanic. He doesn't know where you live, so you must stand outside in the rain with your car. You begin to wonder how you can explain this to your boss. Then you remember that you said you would be in early.

Feel distressed? In most instances, this kind of morning would ruin most persons' day, for it sets a tone that most of us would permit to dominate us.

By contrast, think of a lovely morning at the beach. The clouds are just right and you smell the salty air, while a few seagulls fly overhead.

Notice the difference? We all know that our thoughts can change our heartbeat and pulse rate. We know that we can intensify pain or diminish it.

We know all of this, but how often do we let our thoughts ruin our day, our life?

It is important for all persons to know, and use, the power of mind, the power of thoughts. However, it is most important for alcoholic women, because we must make a special effort to use our minds in the right way. We must not only overcome our negative thoughts, but we must constantly build positive images of ourselves. We must create our new self in mind first.

Drinking is a reaction to our feelings of inadequacy. It is a substitute for our inability to cope with life. We are overwhelmed by our feelings of being incapable, of being bored, of being lonely, of feeling frustrated, of feeling trapped, of feeling useless, of feeling guilty, of actually being emotionally deprived.

Severe negative emotions rule us and we drink. Finally, our drinking becomes a real and severe illness. No longer do we drink to overcome our negative feelings. We drink because we must, because we lost control.

When drinking has ended, we still are faced with the poor image we have of ourselves. We can no longer drink to run away from it so we must repair it. And we do this by learning the secret of mind power, the secret of creating a new self that will provide us with a happy sobriety. Now we can begin to enjoy ourselves through our new knowledge of life. Fulfillment of what we desire in life depends upon what we think of ourselves.

6. *"Life Can Be Ordinary or It Can Be Great"*
For persons other than alcoholics, this statement would probably seem ridiculous. But for us, it is a necessary adjunct, because we are guilty of not having paid much attention to the quality of our lives. We have not respected the living of life as much as we should have. We thought little about the character of life. We are even guilty of sometimes bemoaning the fate of our lives by saying, "Why me?"

Although we only get a one-way ticket through life, we speed over the miles as if we will make the trip many times, as if planning to enjoy it on a later trip. We live as if there is an endless amount of tomorrows.

With sobriety, our perception of life changes. When we stop drinking, we often go through a period of feeling not fully alive; we wonder what life is all about and whether sobriety is worth it. We would go back to drinking again but there is too much pain involved, too much heartbreak. So we feel trapped by this lifeless feeling, this feeling of "what's the use, what's it all about anyway?"

This is the period when growth must take place or sobriety will always be a burden. It is the period when we learn that we get from life what we put into it. Anyone can live and let life just happen, but those who know the secret will plunge in and make life happen.

Making life into something more than just an ordinary experience is to enjoy many individual moments. It is being aware of the present moment and making it come alive.

To make life great is to make each moment come alive. It means investment of self. Drinking removed quality from our lives. Drinking canceled our ever knowing the joy of life, of living.

Sobriety is a happy experience for those who invest in each moment, each day.

7. *"Love Can Change the Course of My World"*

Love is very often difficult for the woman with a drinking problem. Too often she sealed herself away from others because she was forced to remove herself bodily and emotionally when drinking. When not drinking, she is afraid to trust love, to give it or receive it. Loving is a stranger and is elusive.

It is often said that we learn to love by loving, a kind of on-the-job training. Eric Hoffer says, "It is easier to love humanity as a whole than to love one's neighbor."

Probably we are all willing to love and we agree with the premise that love can change the course of our world. But it's the doing it that's tough, because we must reveal ourselves, we must give of ourselves and not be afraid if rejection follows. Are we afraid to love because we might be turned away? Are we afraid to believe that others love us, because we have such a poor opinion of ourselves?

We want love, we yearn for it. Who doesn't? But we are often unable to accept it because of not trusting it, fearing that it will suddenly be withdrawn or that the expression of it is not valid, not earned.

Love has changed the world for these many centuries. We need only look around us to see what love has accomplished; or, for that matter, we can look around us and see what hate has destroyed.

Love is a powerful force. It can change worlds and we

must act to change our own world. We must begin to believe that love has that much power for us.

Ethel Barrymore once wrote, "You must learn day by day, year by year, to broaden your horizon. The more things you love, the more you are interested in, the more you enjoy, the more you are indignant about—the more you have left when anything happens."

8. *"The Fundamental Object of Life Is Emotional and Spiritual Growth"*

Perhaps this should be two statements but it is my belief that with emotional growth, spiritual growth follows. We grow in mind and heart.

Emotional growth comes from frequent introspection with an eye toward changing for the better. Emotional growth comes from the extraction of useful self-knowledge from traumatic situations.

Continued emotional growth prevents unhappiness. It provides us with a course of life to be pursued. It shows us the way to emotional peace and calm. We learn the value of self-control and self-understanding.

Spiritual growth is our reason for being, for existing. It is the essence of life. It is knowing that all we take with us when we leave this earth is what we have become while here. Perhaps spiritual growth is more complicated, for we now move into soul involvement. Spiritual growth is something more assimilated than emotional growth. It is the step beyond, but it follows as night the day.

Spiritual growth is an individual experience, for what is spiritual to me may not be for you. The end result of spiritual growth is inner peace and calm, a knowing one's place in the scheme of the universe, of feeling a relationship to all things and to something greater than ourselves.

I feel spiritual in the observation of nature, for then my spirit floats free and joins in an otherworldly force. I feel a oneness with the universe. I especially feel this oneness when I watch dawn or sunset.

An eighteenth-century metaphysical poet suggested we

see the world in a grain of sand. The microcosm represents the macrocosm as surely as we represent the world, each of us.

9. *"The Past Is Gone Forever"*
For me, I can only say "hurrah!" I want it gone forever. Life is centered in the now, in the present moment. We keep the past only if we perpetuate it, keep recalling it, keep reacting to it.

We must liberate ourselves from what was in order to be free for what is. We must remember that what is will soon be what was. So the real issue is how we handle ourselves in the present moment.

Of course, there will be times when we must extract from our past so that we might learn from it. There will be times when we must examine our emotions of anger and guilt so that they can be dismissed. DISMISSED.

Our only interest in the past is for it to act as a guide, a map, for what we want to avoid in the future.

When I was drinking, I was forever looking forward to something in the future, or I was reciting something from the past. I was never in the present. I was escaping that.

It is important for us to learn why we ran from the present. What we do not need to do is constantly dwell on it, for our ugly feelings will continue to return. We must learn the "why" and move on to life and the living of it. Life is for living, not for recalling.

Living in the past is the fastest way to bankrupt ourselves emotionally. People who live in the past must give way to those who move toward the future. For most women alcoholics, thinking about the past awakens regret. This is an emotion we can ill afford.

The past is gone forever. Today we begin a new life, one that will erase the old, for we are now in charge of ourselves. We master and dictate our actions and lives. We are free from the regret of yesterdays.

10. *"All Love Given Returns Twofold"*
There is nothing very mysterious about the sentiment of

this statement. It is similar to an earlier one, but this is with more direction and more emphatic.

Giving and receiving love is a tough assignment for alcoholic women. We are a frightened group from past experiences. We are wary and, sometimes, crippled in a way that we simply cannot give, or receive, love. We must learn how. We must practice.

The practice begins with our believing in ourself. We must accept the role of responsibility for our actions and emotions. Then we are capable of love, of giving so that we will know the joy of receiving.

We are women reaching out to others by way of our new self-awareness, which tells us that we are amply capable of giving love and we are able to receive love.

We must begin with loving each other in a real feeling of oneness. This means overcoming distrust of each other, for we have a common bond as women, and in our case, as women bonded together by the same illness.

Let us begin to practice this statement in our group setting, for within the group we are better able to know each other. We are able to express our caring for the problems of another. We are able to give love, caring, kindness and compassion. By our giving, we will receive.

So often I am asked, "Who provides the group therapy?" We provide it for ourselves. We are our own counselors for the present and our own physicians for the past. We are these because we love each other and want to help. We give love and it is continually returning to be used over and over again.

Love keeps us alive and wanting to live. It is the wellspring of spirit.

11. *"Enthusiasm Is My Daily Exercise"*

Enthusiasm is as infectious as a new viral strain. Let one woman in a room have it and everyone gets it. It spreads freely, never caring who gets it or what the results might be.

Of course we all know that whatever we feel affects all

persons around us. When we are depressed, our gloom spreads to others and they promptly leave us alone. Who could blame them for leaving us?

Enthusiasm draws people to us, rather than sending them away. It acts like a magnet, probably because so few persons are enthusiastic. It is a rare sight.

The world belongs to those who are enthusiastic. They make it a pleasant place in which we can live, for they add a dash of inspiration. They savor each moment and extract the best from it. They vibrate with life.

Enthusiasm gives life a special meaning. Emerson once wrote, "Nothing great was ever achieved without enthusiasm."

Enthusiasm adds fire to life and it provides the force for accomplishment of all things, most especially good relationships with other persons.

Learn to be enthusiastic about everything. Find something in everything to be enthusiastic about. It's there, just for the looking.

Have you ever known a person who can make shopping for an onion a rich experience? These persons have unlocked a secret that produces the gold nuggets of life.

Our statement says to make enthusiasm a daily exercise. It must be practiced to be achieved. Eventually, it will become a part of you that is always with you. But work at it each day until it becomes a natural instinct.

12. *"I Am a Competent Woman and Have Much to Give Others"*
This statement is one of the final blocks in the building of our new self. It is a cornerstone of our new life, for it makes us declare ourselves: "I am a competent woman . . ."

This is true, you know. Probably you don't know it, because you are afraid to believe it, yet each of us is uniquely different and each of us is capable of something that no one else can do as well.

Alcoholic women are intelligent and hypersensitive, overly generous, overly conscientious, easily overcome with guilt and depression. And alcoholic women are highly competent when they believe it!

The negative emotions experienced by alcoholic women tend to cloud over any sense of belief in self. These negative emotions make us have little regard for ourselves. We permit ourselves to feel unimportant, unneeded and unworthy.

Perhaps society's attitude toward the alcoholic woman has had some part in giving us this feeling. Perhaps we have created this image all by ourselves with the aid of alcohol.

Why mull over the reasons why we do not believe in ourselves? We are capable women when we permit ourselves to be. We are capable of great accomplishment, but we can only reach this fulfillment when we have a complete belief in ourselves and our capacities for accomplishment, for personal fulfillment.

This is our true liberation from alcohol and its effects. We must be liberated from the baggage of self-denial about ourselves and our abilities. We must throw away feelings of guilt, feelings of despair and unworthiness.

Dorothy Day once wrote, "No one has a right to sit down and feel hopeless. There is too much work to do."

Our first assignment is to begin with ourselves. We must begin each day with the absolute and unshakable belief in our own competency. A large part of the Women for Sobriety philosophy is that we must have a clear-cut idea of what we want to be and then, by holding that idea firmly in mind, we will become it. First the thought, then the reality. A woman cannot become what she has not clearly believed in her mind, her thoughts. Act competent. Know that you are.

We are all creatures of habit. Who does not know how easy it is to acquire a bad habit? And how is it done? By doing the same thing over and over. Then it becomes second nature. This can also be true of good habits. Do something over and over, like acting competently, and it will become a habit.

Think good and substantial thoughts. They will become actions.

13. "I Am Responsible for Myself and My Sisters"

This statement represents the culmination of our upward striving for emotional maturity. We cannot feel the responsibility for others until we feel, and accept, the responsibility for ourselves and our actions.

We create ourselves through our actions. We also create our emotions, good and bad, positive and negative.

Since we do create ourselves, we must accept the responsibility for what we have created.

The program of Women for Sobriety as set forth in the thirteen statements of acceptance is a program of mind development through which we create new habits and a new life, a new way of living. This is necessary, because our former way of living did not work, because we had to use drinking to supplement life. Just to stop drinking now is not enough. We must change, find a new way of life.

We cannot help others until we have learned how to help ourselves. But we must move toward the acceptance of the responsibility for other women suffering in the same way we once did. It means that we are to accept her plight as part of our own recovery through self-discovery. Our own real recovery is proportional to our feeling for other women who need us. All religions recognize the necessity for each of us to help others as a way of helping ourselves.

Our responsibility for others, our caring for women who need our emotional support also helps us to feel a new confidence of self. We experience a good feeling about ourselves, something that has often been significantly missing from our lives for a very long time.

This program shows a way of thinking, a way to a new life, a program that is based upon experience . . . my experience. It will work for anyone who wishes to find a new life, one of confidence in self and responsibility to others.

Perhaps the best way I can describe a Women for Sobriety group meeting is to say that it is a conversation that takes place in a circle. Maybe not all meetings are held this way, but I have found that when women are in a circle, there is more informality, more ease with speaking and exchanging thoughts. The meeting is also less threatening to the woman who has just finished with drinking. Speech flows more easily.

The ideal number of women is six to eight, but I seriously doubt that many groups are this ideal number. At least, the ones I have visited have all had more than this number. With eight women, each one has several chances to express herself on whatever topic is being discussed. To keep one woman from monopolizing the conversation, a real no-no, some groups employ the use of an egg timer. Any woman may speak as often as she wants to, but each time she must confine it to three minutes. This makes each woman more conscious of putting her real thoughts up front. Of course, should a woman choose not to speak, this is perfectly all right. She need never speak. However, the problem is usually the other way around.

Keeping the conversation on the track is usually the most difficult part of all meetings. This is one of the few reasons a "leader" is needed, to keep the conversation from drifting. Actually, keeping the conversation from drifting is the responsibility of the entire group.

Women for Sobriety meetings are loosely structured. They are opened with the reading of the Statement of Purpose and are closed with a statement that affirms purpose. With joined hands, women affirm, "We are capable and confident, caring and compassionate, always willing to help another, bonded together in overcoming our disease of alcoholism." Following this a donation is taken, which pays for the group's expenses; the remainder is sent to headquarters. Here again we follow the common practice of AA, except that their meetings are closed with members saying the Lord's Prayer. Like AA, Women for Sobriety wishes to be independent and self-supporting. This can take place only when women feel united in a common cause and unite behind this organization as being their own.

Most groups meet once a week, although I know of some that meet as often as three times a week. That is up to each individual group. Meetings should never last longer than one and a half hours. Beyond that point, the meeting is no longer effective. Here again I know of groups that do meet longer than the suggested period, but that is their decision.

So often I am asked what is discussed at meetings. Our monthly newsletter, *Sobering Thoughts*, carries four subjects for each month's meetings. These provide the substance for the meetings. One of the four subjects is always one of our thirteen statements so that at least one meeting each month is devoted to the basic program and to a discussion of how each woman uses that particular statement. Other subjects written about are: "Doubt and Fear," "Resentments," "Sexual Identification," "The Woman Alcoholic," "The Joy of Living in the Now," "Woman's Role," "Meditation," "Depression," and so on. All women subscribe to the newsletter and take it with them to meetings.

Women for Sobriety meetings are often begun in a woman's home before moving to more public quarters. Sometimes it will take a few weeks for the meeting to "jell," but then it should be moved somewhere else, preferably to a community room in one of the new bank buildings or a meeting place in a shopping mall. We have had an excellent response to groups that meet in the new shopping malls, especially those that meet early on a Saturday afternoon. Women find it extremely easy to get away from home and to a meeting merely by saying "I'll be at the Plymouth Meeting Mall for a short while." Funny isn't it, how we sneak around life because of what others think? Do they make us do it? Or do we do it to ourselves?

Often I am asked "What about anonymity?" Since many of our women belong to AA, they are firm in their commitment to anonymity and, as far as Women for Sobriety is involved, that is always honored. Anonymity is entirely up to each individual woman and each woman must respect what others desire for themselves. Recently we find many women coming forward and speaking out, accepting their disease as simply a treatable disease that needs to be recognized as a health problem. Of course, there is still stigma attached to being a woman alcoholic but it seems to be lessening, even if very slowly. It will be removed when more of us speak out. However, I understand and respect those women who want to remain anonymous.

Another question asked is "Am I an alcoholic?" In Women for Sobriety groups we do not spend any time on the semantics of whether or not one is an alcoholic. Everyone present has a problem with alcohol. She no longer is able to drink, for, when she does, her drinking gets out of control. It may have been that she once had another problem and the use of alcohol helped to alleviate the pain of that other problem. But then dependence upon alcohol became so great, it became the problem. We must work at solving both problems through a change in ourselves.

The object of Women for Sobriety groups is to lead all of us to a new philosophy of life, since the way we approached life before was not practical. However, even if we change our way of thinking and the way of approaching problems, physiologically we are never able to drink again, for we would be right back into drinking without control.

As an ideal, Women for Sobriety envisions each woman growing and maturing to a point where she may not have to have dependence upon lifelong meetings, but if this is the way she is able to meet life's problems and challenges, Women for Sobriety groups will be everywhere for her to attend. But the ideal is emotional and spiritual growth, which leads one away from all dependence. Women for Sobriety groups never hear entire drinking histories. Patterns of behavior while drinking may sometimes be referred to but never an entire life history of drinking.

Our drinking days are over. We must now embark on the formation of a life-style that copes with problems utilizing dependence upon self and not upon a drug. We begin to see that our actions are our responsibility and whatever happens to us was brought on by ourselves. We permit ourselves to know joy, happiness, depression, sadness, anger, resentment, discouragement, etc. We are the author of the script by which we live our lives. We are confident or not; we are in control or not; we see options or we give in; we act or react; we are what we think and what *we permit*. Daily I recommit myself to this.

How to use the Women for Sobriety program? Each woman should arise twenty minutes earlier than her regular schedule.

She should find a quiet place and observe Nature for several minutes. Then, in the stillness of the morning, go over every one of the Thirteen Statements of Acceptance, thinking through each one clearly. Then, one statement should be selected and used that day . . . lived and exercised. Then thoughts should be turned to our place in life. We must think about our relationship to all things . . . trees, bushes, plants, people, events.

In our quiet hours we must realize that our lives are but a moment in time. All we take with us when we leave this earth is what we have become. Accumulation of money and property, success as we know it, is of little value if we have not managed the success of our inner selves and our relation to other things.

If the Women for Sobriety program is nothing else, it is a pathway into one's own consciousness. It is our awareness with ourselves that makes the difference between being drunk or sober. It is the acceptance of our responsibility for our actions and the results of those actions that makes for long-lasting sobriety.

Daily we receive letters from women who ask if they are alcoholics. Signs of alcoholism are most often displayed in subtle ways, for the woman who is well on her way to becoming an alcoholic drinks in a different way from others. Questions such as: Do you drink before going to a party? Do you drink to get through the day? Do you always drink to drunkenness? Do you have trouble remembering all of what happened the night before? Do you ever have a drink in the morning to recover? An affirmative answer to any of these questions indicates that this woman needs help and should seek out a Women for Sobriety group by writing to us.

Perhaps all women who belong to Women for Sobriety are not alcoholics. They are, however, women who have a problem with alcohol. Hopefully, Women for Sobriety will serve not only as an organization that helps with recovery but also plays just as large a part in prevention of alcoholism. All our members have one thing in common: they have stopped drinking and are looking for a new way to approach problems and a new way to find fulfillment of emotional needs.

Every group at some time or another has to wrestle with the

problem of women who come to meetings who are still drinking. Each group must settle this individually. One group I know of had a woman who continued to come for many weeks, and she always disrupted the group meeting, so that, finally, the group asked her never to come back. It was obvious that the woman had no intention of stopping drinking. She wanted to drink but wanted to give up the suffering.

You may be wondering where there is a group for you to join. Obviously a list of groups cannot appear in this book. We have found that, because we are so new, many newspaper people try many different ways of trying to find a group so that a picture of a meeting can be taken. Should any group desire that, it is their decision, but here at headquarters our duty is to protect each group. Any woman who desires information about how to join or how to start a group needs only to write to Quakertown, Pennsylvania 18951. Women for Sobriety is constantly growing, a growth usually proportionate to exposure. However, our exposure has, at times, outrun our ability to keep up with group formation. (This is where our lack of funds is most destructive, for we desperately need field representatives to help groups get started. In cities like Chicago, New York, Minneapolis, and Los Angeles women like Lynnette Given, Rita Zimmer, Kathleen Komaridis, and Janet Glassock, have given tirelessly of themselves.) Our great need is for women with several years of sobriety to come forward and say "Send me the names of the women in my area and I'll start a group." Do you qualify?

In time, of course, Women for Sobriety groups will be as numerous and as far-flung as are AA groups, so that women everywhere will have a group to attend within close proximity. Soon, too, the Women for Sobriety program will be used in many, many more facilities than that number already using it. It should, and will, take its place beside AA in offering simply another, and additional, way to sobriety and a new life.